Effective Learning in Classrooms

D0246373

This book addresses the central issue of classrooms, and the issue which is too seldom addressed: learning. We do not mean teaching, we do not mean performance, we do not mean 'work'. This book is *really* about learning in classrooms, what makes learning effective and how it may be promoted in classrooms.

This book takes the special context of the classroom seriously, not only because of its effects on teachers and pupils, but because classrooms are notorious as contexts which change little. Readers will not be offered yet more tips, but real thinking and evidence based on what we know about how classrooms change. Four major dimensions of promoting effective learning in classrooms are handled in depth.

Throughout the book there are two forms of evidence: evidence from practising teachers in the form of case studies and examples, and evidence from international research in the form of useful ideas and frameworks.

Chris Watkins is a reader in education and Drs Carnell and Lodge are senior lecturers at the University of London Institute of Education. They have been course leaders for the MA in Effective Learning, the MA in School Effectiveness and School Improvement, and the Advanced Diploma in Learning and Teaching. They have also led a range of projects with schools and local authorities, all of which focus on learning.

Effective Learning
in Classrooms

Chris Watkins, Eileen Carnell and
Caroline Lodge

P·C·P

Paul Chapman
Publishing

First published 2007

 Paul Chapman Publishing
A SAGE Publications Company
1 Oliver's Yard
55 City Road
London
EC1Y 1SP

SAGE Publications Inc
2455 Teller Road
Thousand Oaks, California 91320

SAGE Publications India Pvt Ltd
B1/I1 Mohan Cooperative Industrial Area
Mathura Road, New Delhi 110 044
India

SAGE Publications Asia-Pacific Pte Ltd
33 Pekin Street #02-01
Far East Square
Singapore 048763

Library of Congress Control Number: 2006933407

A catalogue record for this book is available from the British Library

ISBN: 978-1-4129-0070-6 (hbk)
ISBN: 978-1-4129-0071-3 (pbk)

Typeset by Dorwyn, Wells, Somerset
Printed in Great Britain by Athenaeum Press, Gateshead
Printed on paper from sustainable resources

Contents

List of Tables and Figures

Preface

Why this Book?

To our knowledge this is the only book for teachers which:
- takes seriously the complexity of the classroom
- understands the way that classroom practices do (and do not) change
- is based on a twenty first century understanding of learning
- offers a comprehensive range of suggestions for classroom practice
- is evidence-rich in two senses: research evidence and professional evidence.

Who are the Authors?

This book is written by three colleagues who, amongst other things, have recently been leading the following courses at the University of London Institute of Education:

MA in Effective Learning
MA in School Effectiveness and School Improvement
Professional Diploma in Learning and Teaching

These are not dry academic courses – quite the opposite. Many teachers from the UK and all over the world who take them describe them as challenging and re-professionalising.

The authors also lead projects and short courses with many teachers, schools and local authorities in England and Wales.

Between them their experience as professional educators amounts to about a hundred years – and never the same one twice.

Why Now?

The contents of this book would be appropriate at any time, but in England and other countries there is an extra reason which is current: many classrooms have reverted to a form of operation which is centuries old and which does not prepare young people for the world we live in now. Surveys suggest that a teaching-dominated form has increased in recent years, with a correspondingly passive role for learners. This is not the way to get the high performance, which we all want for all young people, as one of the things they take away from school.

Effective learning is a core process in many domains of life, and school can play a special part in helping learners develop the approaches and understandings which will be effective across their learning landscape.

An Outline Map of the Book

The context of the classroom affects a great deal of what teachers and pupils do. It crucially affects the approaches to learning which are adopted. Yet the context of the classroom is rarely addressed when practices for classrooms are suggested by many proponents. Instead of replicating this, we embed our understandings of effective learning in what is known about classrooms.

Part I (Chapters 1 to 5) engages with your experience and your understanding of classrooms, especially in identifying the processes which have been at work when learning has been best in classrooms you know. Then we seek to analyse how classrooms are seen, in order to identify the tensions that teachers face, and the issues when teachers resolve these tensions in a non-traditional way for the purposes of promoting effective learning.

Part II (Chapters 6 to 10) aims to extend your experience with frameworks and ideas from a range of sources, mainly using four headings which regularly arise in teachers' and pupils' accounts of the best learning in classrooms. In this part of the book we use a greater balance of evidence from research, because we want no-one to think that these frameworks are not solidly based on dependable evidence. There has been too much advice and instruction to teachers which are based more on ideology than evidence. The last chapter in this section examines the process of assessment and what may be done in classroom practices to reclaim assessment for effective learning.

Part III (Chapter 11) encourages you to take forward the enquiries and experiments which are appropriate for you in classrooms that you know. This will entail doing some things which are not part of the dominant picture in classrooms today, so we encourage you to be exceptional in both senses of the word.

We aim for this book to be thought-provoking, challenging and practically useful. We sincerely hope that you and the pupils you learn with enjoy reclaiming the energy of learning.

PART I

YOUR CONTEXT AND YOUR EXPERIENCE

Learning in Classrooms – What's the Best We Know?

Learning from the Best of our Experience

To begin this book and this chapter we invite you to initiate an 'appreciative inquiry' (Hammond, 2000) in order to introduce the themes of this book. Appreciative inquiry is an approach to innovation or improvement that starts by identifying the best of what currently is. It takes the stance that in every organisation something works well, and that we would be well advised to learn from it and take it into our future. Participants are asked to identify how 'the best of what currently is' came about, and work at imagining what it would be like if there were more. Then if we work out how these best experiences came about, we can identify what will be needed for more to happen.

We have used this approach to think about promoting more effective learning in classrooms. In every classroom something works well. It is important to identify these aspects:

To notice when 'best' learning happens in classrooms.
To pick up a range of creative perspectives including those of young people in classrooms.
To remind ourselves of our own achievements in contributing to effective learning in classrooms.
To appreciate young people's roles and potentials.
To carry forward into the future the best parts of our past.

> Take a few minutes to think about a classroom you know in which the sense of learning has been really positive. Maybe there has been engagement, excitement, reflection, an 'ah-ha' moment …
>
>   When you have identified the situation do all you can to reconstruct it in your mind's eye – recall the room, the conditions, the people and so on. Capture the concrete details of the things that made that experience possible. If possible, share this with someone else.

You might find yourself identifying such things as:

- Learners drove the agenda.
- There was real help going on between the pupils.
- They were active.
- People were taking thoughtful risks and weren't afraid of making mistakes.
- I stood back and the students ran with it.

Appreciative inquiry is not the usual way of approaching improvement. It contrasts with problem solving and action planning when the question asked is 'What is the problem here and what are we going to do about it?' It is a positive approach that does not seek to find fault or emphasise negative aspects. It encourages people to build on existing success, building on the idea that people have usually lived some part of their dream.

A further part of the activity involves participants in drawing up 'provocative propositions': these are statements which build on their best experience of effective learning and provoke thinking to go forward. These statements help them to imagine what it would be like if the future of learning in classrooms was more effective, and what they might have to contribute.

Here are some examples from our experience.

> Children learn best …
>   when they take responsibility for their own learning
>   when they are actively engaged in their learning
>   when learning is interactive (as opposed to passive or seat-work)
>   when they see themselves as successful learners.

These statements were produced by the staff of a primary school. If we look in more depth at the statements we can see that the teachers believed that the best learning in schools occurs in classrooms where it is active, social, involves learner responsibility and the young people have awareness of themselves as learners. The statements may not seem very provocative (in the sense of being challenging or surprising); indeed some people have commented that they are self-evident (we wish they were!). Perhaps this is because they are the outcome of group deliberations rather than unique individual experiences. However, these teachers were identifying things they needed to work at to improve learning in classrooms in their school. In fact they used them to shape a project on learning.

Other examples we have collected from teachers include:

Effective learning …
  occurs when the teacher is invisible
  happens when people are willing to be vulnerable
  occurs when students take an active role in their learning experiences
  happens after failure
  does not need a teacher to give students knowledge
  happens when the teacher throws out her plans
  is when classroom management brings about a positive atmosphere where students want to learn.

You might find yourself provoked by some of these statements, and it is worth reflecting on your own reaction, alongside another reflection on what might have prompted the teachers to make these statements. For example, we found ourselves commenting that the final statement is more about teachers' activities than learning, and suggests that young people only want to learn when it is managed by their teachers. The statement suggests something about the conditions and context in which the teacher making that proposition was working. Our reactions tell you something about our views of learning.

We also noticed that a number of these statements suggested a less didactic role for teachers than is common. And a couple look at vulnerability and failure, and point to the importance of feelings in learning.

What provocative propositions would you make as a result of your engagement in the activity above?

What would be the most provocative propositions you could make about learning in classrooms known to you and your colleagues?

What does your proposition say about your view of learning and the conditions in which you are promoting learning?

Further dialogue between teachers is likely to promote more widespread understanding about learning in classrooms.

Who would you like to engage in dialogue?

Another element in this book will be to encourage you to undertake enquiries with learners about issues which affect their learning. And we regularly receive evidence that the view from pupils affirms the thoughts that teachers have. For example, a school in West London surveyed all the pupils about a range of things to do with school and learning. From the very many things that were said, here is a brief selection. Perhaps some of the themes connect to what is emerging for you.

Year Group	What do you like about how you learn at school?	What would you like to see included?
Reception	Choosing	Choosing (2)
Year 1	Reading books to find out	Golden Time
	Investigation	
	Hands on	
Year 2	Reading to find out	More time for reading
	Choices	More time to finish
		Choosing activities
Year 3	Project work	Free time
Year 4	Experiments	
Year 5	Independent ICT learning	
Year 6	Sit where we want	
	Not stopping at the end of 45 minutes	More free choice

What do you think of these comments from some pupils? Does their perspective overlap with yours?

Looking Ahead

The kinds of issues that we hope are raised for you by the appreciative inquiry are the kinds of issues we deal with in-depth in this book. We now outline the themes that we have found that excite, interest and intrigue teachers. These have emerged through involvement with teachers and young people as we have engaged with them through Masters and Diplomas courses, in projects with schools focused on learning, in research with young people and teachers and in writing for various audiences over the years. These themes have emerged through our writing and conversations and deep reflection together about learning.

Views of effective learning in classrooms

It is a key point of this book that various different views of what will count for effective learning in classrooms exist around us, and that these importantly different views are rarely analysed. You might have noticed something about your own view as a result of devising a provocative proposition from the appreciative activity above. Here is one view of learning that you might want to compare with your own:

> How do people learn except through pressure and threat? (Chris Woodhead, formerly the Chief Inspector of Schools in England, writing in *The Spectator* in 1995.)

Different conceptions of learning are outlined in the next chapter. We begin to describe our case for learning that involves activity, collaboration, learner agency and meta-learning (learning about learning). Our stance contrasts with views such as that of the former Chief Inspector above.

When we look at classrooms what do we see?

We trace conceptions of learning in classrooms, including through drawings and photographs by children, and notice the dominance of a particular view of learning. We notice that this view of learning – a teacher-centred, passive model – is not necessarily effective today.

What other discourses influence teachers?

We consider external and internal influences on learning in classrooms, and how the effects of a focus on performance in tests, ideas about the curriculum and assessment, about fixed ability, trends and fads, all conspire to reinforce conditions that can work against effective learning.

When people work against the grain

In our work we are fortunate to learn with teachers who find the resources to work against the dominant influences and who promote effective learning in their classrooms. In Chapter 5 we present three examples to identify the factors that supported teachers in promoting more effective learning. For example, it seems important in schools to make learning and learning about learning part of the public discourse.

Promoting activity, collaboration, agency and meta-learning in the classroom

The following chapters examine in more depth the strategies used by teachers working against the grain. They promote increased active learning, collaboration, agency (young people driving the agenda and process of their learning) and meta-learning (helping young people understand their own learning).

Reclaiming assessment

We include ideas about the way in which assessment can promote effective learning and we use the four themes of the previous chapters to illustrate the relationship between effective learning and classroom assessment practices.

Being exceptional

The book ends by honouring the experiences and voices of teachers and students and by noticing what enabled them to be exceptional. We invite you to express your vision for your classroom and to take part in reclaiming and celebrating your professional voice in classrooms and staffrooms.

What is Effective Learning in Classrooms?

We now set out what we mean by effective learning, and start by considering different conceptions of learning. Ideas about meta-cognition and meta-learning are then examined. This will be related to learning in classrooms. We will pay attention to different cultural constructions of learning, that is, what learning may mean in different countries, cultures and contexts. To do this we will draw on our experiences of working with teachers from all over the world.

In the last chapter you undertook an appreciative inquiry of effective learning in a classroom. We presented some provocative propositions that we have collected from teachers undertaking this task. Underpinning each statement, and indeed implicit in teachers' and learners' activities, are beliefs and theories about how people learn. This section will introduce some conceptions of learning to help illuminate beliefs about learning drawn from research and your own experiences.

Conceptions of Learning

Take a moment to make a note of the first three words or phrases that come into your head when you think about what learning is. A number of research projects have investigated people's understandings of learning, showing that the word 'learning' has different meanings for different people. Marton et al. (1993) report the following hierarchy of meanings gathered from some Open University students. They referred to them as 'everyday conceptions of learning':

- getting more knowledge
- memorising and reproducing
- applying facts or procedures
- understanding
- seeing something in a different way
- changing as a person.

How does your response relate to the ones on this list? Are the words and phrases you thought of similar to one of them, or do they differ, and why might this be?

Different conceptions may be held by different people or by the same person in different circumstances and for different purposes. We notice that all the conceptions in Marton et al.'s list tend to imply learning as an individual activity. We also notice that the list begins with a mechanical view of learning: taking in or consuming more information. This is enshrined in the idea that to possess knowledge is to be brainy, a view which is quite common in everyday life and beliefs. 'Brain of Britain' is a general knowledge quiz on the radio, and children reflect the idea that knowledge is central when they say their teachers ought to know everything about their subject. The popular view can be resistant to change even in the face of children being able to find out what they need for themselves when they want to, for example by searching the internet. The conception of 'learning as getting more knowledge' also suggests that this knowledge is separate from the individual and to be consumed or banked. One teacher talked in these terms about the enthusiasm for learning shown by a class of 8 year-olds:

> In my class the more you give them that they haven't had before, the more they grab it. They eat it up if it's something new. I mean, my classes, I've been very lucky, they seem to be like that, they just eat all knowledge. (Lodge, 2002: field notes)

Usha, an 8 year-old girl in another school, used the image of getting things into your head or your brain: this is a common view among young people when asked about good learning:

> As soon as someone teaches you then you feel like you've got something else you know and it's like it's going to be locked up in your brain. (Lodge, 2002: field notes)

In this conception of learning, people's ways of talking about a 'good learner' emphasise things like memorising, and the evaluation of learning is seen as outside the person – it's about performance and compliance: someone completes their work which can then be evaluated with ticks and marks:

> Yes, like you're doing the work, and get all the ticks, and they've memorised all the work, and they've known all the sums, their times tables. (8 year-old boy: Lodge, 2002: field notes)

Here we can see that the approach to assessment may generate this conception of learning. We return to the influence of assessment in Chapters 4 and 10.

Further down Marton et al.'s list is 'applying facts and procedures'. We hear this conception when teachers say they value learning that enables children to apply their knowledge in different circumstances. One 14 year-old boy gave another example when he contrasted the first aid course he had recently taken with an English lesson on *Othello*:

> And you feel happy with yourself because you know you have learned something that you can use. Personally, this stuff about Iago, once we've finished the subject I'm never going to use it again in my life but first aid is always going to be useful. (Lodge, 2002).

The list of conceptions moves on to include seeing learning as making meaning, interpreting events and constructing knowledge or understanding. For example, one young person expressed his conception of learning in this way:

> Learning is what I do as a human, to become a better human. How can exams test really important learning, like learning to love someone, or learning to cope when that person dies? I will try to stop beating myself up about not getting 'A' grades in exams because I think I have more to offer to the world than the sum total of my school exam results. (12 year-old student: Williams, 2002)

We were impressed by this exceptional view of learning: the student is in a high-performing school, but it is about more than performance, it is about core human experiences and making a contribution.

The last conception 'changing as a person' should not be taken to mean 'all at once'! It can refer to a change in cognitive, social or emotional states. Gill, a 14 year-old student said "I think when you have a good learning experience it makes you feel better for the rest of the day" (Lodge, 2002). And one teacher who had been investigating learning with her science class of 8 year-olds described how it felt to be a different person:

> I felt the joy and exhilaration of a new teacher who encounters many fresh experiences without ever feeling like a novice. I am now a committed learner. (Ann Pilmoor, teacher-researcher quoted in Carnell and Lodge, 2002a: 67)

The crucial point about conceptions of learning is that they are influential, not just 'in the head' ideas, or merely academic. Someone's conception of learning has a big influence on what they do, how they go about their learning. Doubtless every teacher has experienced this in their interactions with pupils: some pupils display their conception of learning by implying that the responsibility for their learning rests with you! But we should also remember that conceptions of learning may vary for the same individual, depending on their context. This stops us as teachers thinking that our pupils come with a view of learning that was formed elsewhere and that we have no influence over. Far from it: the influence of the immediate context, for example the classroom, can be very influential.

The Effect of Context

The list of conceptions which Marton et al. provide resulted from research with adults learning at a distance, in the formal setting of a university course, and maybe the balance of their results reflects that context. Learners in other contexts, perhaps including you, may have different conceptions of learning. For example, when we talk with young people about their learning outside school, we often hear more active, experimental and social views than we do when they talk about learning in school. You might have noticed that Marton et al.'s list does not include learning through collaboration and dialogue, building knowledge together with others. Yet schoolchildren will remark on this, when their classroom context has supported it and they have a chance to review. For example:

> Working in a small group in class is really helpful. You hear everyone's ideas and you can say 'no he doesn't agree with me' and why not, and she does and she is sort of half way and it's really good because you understand what you think compared with other people's views. (14 year-old girl: Carnell, 2000)

So our pupils' examples may reflect a richer conception of learning than those included in Marton et al.'s list, depending on what their classroom experiences are like.

We now have considered three key elements, all of which have an influence on each other: an individual's conception of learning, their way of going about learning, and the immediate context of their learning. These are summarised in Figure 2.1, where the wider context is also indicated (and will be discussed later in this chapter). Note that all the arrows indicating influence go in both directions: individuals can be influenced by the context, but they can also influence the context, through their beliefs and actions.

Inquiring into Conceptions and Contexts

There are many ways to inquire into a pupil's conception of learning: informal conversations, listening to conversations between pupil peers, questionnaires of

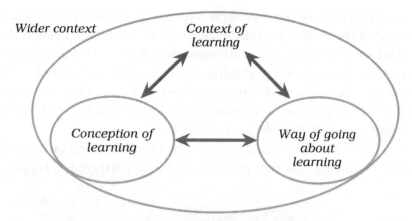

Figure 2.1 Conceptions, actions and context of learning

Note that this diagram could portray the elements and influences for a pupil, but it could equally portray them for a teacher.

various sorts, and open-ended writing. A rich form of enquiry, not depending too much on language, is to ask young people to draw. When asked to draw a good learner we have found that primary school pupils often draw a person with a big head and big ears! Thus they reflect the brainy, consuming, listening conception of learning which was discussed above. But learning is always influenced by context, so rather than invite them to draw a learner, we invite them to draw a learning context. When one of our teacher colleagues asked a young person in a class of 10 year-olds to draw a learning occasion she produced the drawing in Figure 2.2.

Figure 2.2 A 10 year-old's drawing of a learning occasion (Harris, 2002)

This picture is typical of the dominant response in Dean Harris's research. You will notice that the children are sitting in rows, facing the teacher and the blackboard on which is written some sums. Sums were the most frequently drawn element in many drawings. Many children see themselves as isolated, passive and dependent on the teacher for the acquisition of knowledge. Another teacher told us that when her class of 6 year-olds first began to talk about learning, the children said they only learned by listening to her.

Other students will have richer conceptions than those expressed in the dominant view. A drawing that captures some of this is portrayed in Figure 2.3.

Figure 2.3 Another 10 year-old's drawing of a learning occasion (Harris, 2002)

What we notice here is that the learner is not relying on the teacher; the learner is making connections, and learning with friends and family and other adults. There is an assumption that understanding is more significant than the acquisition of knowledge.

So if our inquiries into people's conceptions of learning demonstrate differences, are there some big differences between those views of learning which have been identified?

Models of Learning

A model is not the real thing, but it tries to say something important about the real thing by identifying key elements and describing how they relate to each other. So it is with models of learning. Amongst the very large body of literature on learning, and in surveys of how this literature developed over the last century (Mayer, 2001), it is possible to identify three major models of learning. These are summarised in Table 2.1.

Table 2.1 Three models of learning

Models of learning	
Reception	Concerned with quantity, facts and skills; assumes transmission of knowledge from an external source (e.g. teacher). Emotional and social aspects are not attended to. *Learning = being taught.*
Construction	Concerned with the learner's construction of meaning through discussion, discovery, open-ended learning, making connections. *Learning = individual sense-making.*
Co-construction	Concerned with the learner's construction of meaning through interaction and collaboration with others, especially through dialogue. *Learning = building knowledge with others.*

The important point is that these models are not just found in literature: they are found in everyday talk, in images of learning, in formal documents, and so on. And they are also found in pupils' communications. We suggest that in the drawings above, Figure 2.2 speaks of the reception model, and Figure 2.3 reflects more the construction model. It is not common for young people to draw the third model because they tend to have little experience of that approach and it may therefore seem difficult to represent. But Rosie (aged 6) has experienced a different form of classroom, as shown in her drawing (Figure 2.4). Here we see pupils voicing their own questions – including about learning – and stating that they learn by talking together. It is no coincidence that Rosie draws the pupils seated round a large table: her teacher, Zoe Bonnell, ran her classroom as a learning community, partly on the model by Vasconcelos and Walsh (2001) which emphasises the big table.

Models and Classrooms

Classrooms are very complex contexts, which vary in important ways. One of the ways that classrooms vary is that their practices and ways of working can

Figure 2.4 A 6 year-old's drawing of learning (Bonnell, 2005) "We learn by talking together", "Why are bees black and yellow?", "Why are snakes different?", "How do we learn?"

represent different models of learning. So for each of the three models introduced above, it is possible to imagine how that classroom operates.

On many occasions classrooms are operated on a simple view of learning ('Learning = being taught') with the idea that pupils receive in some simple way what teacher teaches. In England the reception model is the most common in classrooms. The teacher and teaching are dominant. The latter's purpose is often expressed as getting more knowledge 'in their heads'. Assessment is then used to work out whether they did get it in their heads, and focuses on the quantity of knowledge learned and the idea of 'basic' skills. This model is not dominant in all countries, though it probably is in most. Occasionally someone from another country can point this out, as with a visitor from New Zealand who noted that in the classrooms she visited there was plenty of time given to teaching. "When do the children get time for learning?" she asked.

In the second model, construction, the learner is more dominant, and as a result of the shift away from a focus on the teacher, the social context of the classroom is also brought into focus. The purpose is seen as the learner making meaning. In this model 'content' is not for delivery or coverage; it is for connecting with previous knowledge, extending understanding and helping learners to see things in new ways. Assessment in this model may rely partly on knowledge recall, but it also promotes individual interpretation and choice in order to assess understanding.

In the third model, co-construction, the classroom operates in a way where learners create knowledge together, and they may create a collaborative product from this. The teacher acts to encourage opportunities that promote dialogue and other collaborative activities to help the learners together to make sense of their learning experiences. In this model assessment is integrated into the process of learning and may take many forms, including feedback, self- or group-assessment and includes giving a collaborative account of the learning process.

It might be helpful at this stage for you to reflect on familiar classrooms.

- Which models of learning are dominant in your school and in your classrooms?
- To what extent do the teachers in these classrooms promote a particular model of learning?
- What are the factors that influence classroom interactions?

On that last question, we do not underestimate the numerous factors which operate on teachers in current times, many of which can lead to classrooms operating on the first model, reception. When teachers are under pressure (e.g. from exam performance, inspection and observations for judgemental purposes, concerns with behaviours – see for example Sullivan, 2000) teachers tend to become more controlling and promote the first model. Where the pressure includes making teachers 'accountable' for pupils' test results, we also notice what has been described as 'defensive teaching' (McNeil, 1988). We consider these themes further in Chapter 4. But these examples only emphasise some of the distortions in the purpose and context of classrooms, and they do not lead to effective learning.

Effective Learning

Having explored different understandings of learning, we now examine the concept of 'effective learning'. In many countries there has been an emphasis on 'effectiveness' in schools and in education systems, and the word itself has been contentious at times when interpreted in a narrow or mechanical fashion. The same applies when it is attached to learning. It is important to consider what effective learning means, and to ask "Effective for what?" "Effective for when?" This helps us remember that the term 'effective learning' only makes sense when the context of learning and the goals are specified. It helps us recognise that effective learning today is likely to be different from what it would have been a century ago, or in another era of the history of classrooms.

The contemporary context has some important features that mean that the goals of learning need to focus less on knowledge acquisition by individuals and more on knowledge generation with others. The reception model was dominant at a time when it was important for people to learn a finite body of information. While these features vary in their impact in different parts of the world we note the significant effects of the following everywhere:

- More information is available – learners, both adults and young people, need to know how to find and select relevant information, to process it, connect it, use it …
- The capacity to learn and to adapt needs to be lifelong because change is a permanent state.
- Employment requires being able to enhance and transfer knowledge and to operate collaboratively.
- Learning is increasingly taking place in different settings and with different relationships. Learning is a way of being. (Adapted from Watkins et al., 2002)

All over the world effective learning increasingly means more knowledge generation (construction) with others (co-construction), and less independent knowledge acquisition (coverage). This is recognised by an increasing number of governments. For example, in Hong Kong:

> Schools should also encourage students to inquire beyond the confines of 'curriculum prescriptions' and textbooks, and to process information and make their own judgements in order to enhance their knowledge-building capacity. (Hong Kong Education Department, 2002: 78)

And in Singapore, following their 'Thinking Schools, Learning Nation' initiative, the Minister for Education has said "Ironically, being prepared for the knowledge economy does not mean acquiring more knowledge. Instead, a change of paradigm is required." And new policies for secondary schools state:

> The changes will shift the emphasis of education from efficiency to diversity, from content mastery to learning skills, and from knowing to thinking. (Singapore Ministry of Education, 2002)

Another way of saying this is that in every context the nature and pace of change mean that learners need to focus more on *how they learn*, with others, and to be strategic about their learning. We focus in detail on what this means for classrooms in Chapter 9, but we find that teachers already have the core idea, especially when they look in detail at learners they know who seem to be effective.

Effective learners have gained understanding of the individual and social processes necessary to learn how to learn. They have acquired a range of strategies and can monitor and review their learning to gauge the effectiveness of these strategies. This point is especially important, since there are many examples where particular single strategies are sold to schools with claims for promoting learning. But the evidence shows that particular strategies are not effective: they often do not get used or transfered to other contexts. This only happens when a learner can notice, monitor and review how their learning is going. Effective learning includes this vital ingredient of learning about learning or 'meta-learning'.

In Table 2.2 we summarise the main features of effective learning and learners. We explore how the classroom may promote these features in turn in Chapters 6 to 9.

Table 2.2 Effective learning and learners

Effective learning is ...	An effective learner ...
an activity of construction	is active and strategic
handled with (or in the context of) others	is skilled in collaboration
driven by the learner	takes responsibility for their learning
the monitoring and review of the effectiveness of approaches and strategies for the goals and context.	understands her/his learning and plans, monitors and reflects on their learning

Learning is an activity of *making* meaning – construction – not simply of receiving. The social dimension is always present, and in social contexts collaboration supports learning. Effective learning has to be regulated by the learner, not the teacher. These aspects of effective learning are all connected by the fourth feature, meta-learning – being aware of the processes of their learning, how they are learning. Effective learners have learned to monitor their strategies, purposes, outcomes, effects and contexts (Ertmer and Newby, 1996; Sternberg, 2003). In Chapter 5 we will consider in more depth the implications of making changes in classrooms to promote more effective learning, and how these changes can contribute to changes in power, content, roles, responsibility and evaluation (Weimer, 2002).

The Wider Context

We have already briefly mentioned some examples of pressures on teachers from the wider context, and we will explore this in more detail in Chapter 4. But there is a wider influence which we might call the 'wider culture', which also needs to be considered. Here we want to note some themes that appear in a range of countries, and which influence how learning is viewed in classrooms.

In many parts of the world the teacher dominates the classroom. "In Jamaica the teacher is King!" one teacher told us. And pressures on teachers exist in many countries. In different parts of the world the examination system influences what happens in classrooms; for example, there is an emphasis on content and coverage in Greek secondary classrooms where they have annual examinations. In a Jordanian private school, one teacher observed that for younger students the social and extra-curricula activities of the school were regarded as important, but this changed when the girls were faced with examinations.

Classrooms around the world are recognisable on some basic features: there are a number of young people in the same space as one teacher. Some countries (for example, in the UK) organise same-age classes; others (for example, in Nigeria) organise classes according to attainment and not age. In every classroom there is often a physical boundary of some sort. The learners are usually engaged in the same or similar tasks as each other. The furniture is usually arranged so that the learners can write or draw at a table or desk. The desks are usually arranged so that the teacher can see what's happening.

A recent video study in seven countries highlighted other similarities: teachers talked more than students – at least 8:1 teacher to student words; at least 90 per cent of lessons used a textbook or worksheet (Hiebert et al., 2003; see also Stigler and Hiebert, 1998). No one country was distinct on all the features observed.

Alongside these consistent features the experience of young people in classrooms varies across the world in other ways. Variations we have noted in our conversations with teachers helped us to understand a range of influences which aided us in seeing how things can be different and what teachers need to take into account if they are planning changes.

Some of the themes we have noted were:

- Flexibility and routines: the degree to which classroom activities are seen to be in the control of teachers and young people, and the extent to which they are seen as routinised and regularised (usually by external influences).
- Beliefs about learning: for example, that there is a body of knowledge that young people have to absorb in order to progress through the school.
- Beliefs about learners: who has responsibility for the learning; that young people can be categorised and labelled as 'normal', 'gifted' or 'disabled' and then treated accordingly or that young people's intelligence is fixed.
- Assessment and accountability: many assessment systems focus on what is easy to assess. They have not caught up with some of the complexities of learning, such as skills in building knowledge with others. Assessment often triggers a response which reinforces learners' isolation, inactivity and skills in memory and reproduction.

Schools as organisations also affect classrooms in different ways, and the cultural context in different countries can influence how effective an organisation is in promoting learning. The culture of organisations or countries can be considered along similar dimensions. Table 2.3 is derived from Hofstede's (1980) work. He was a Dutch academic, who researched the relationship between 117,000 employees' core values and their practices in many different countries. He used this data to analyse cultures on several dimensions. The degree to which each of these dimensions affects ideas about learning, and about teaching, varies in different contexts, and it would be an oversimplification to assume that one culture pertains uniformly across a nation or a region, or indeed an organisation. The following table adapts Hofstede's dimensions and attempts to map some implications for effective learning in an organisation.

Table 2.3 Hofstede's cultural dimension considered in relation to effective learning

Dimension	Description related to possible impact on learning
Individualism – collectivism	The degree to which the organisation puts value on collaboration as significant in learning for organisations and individuals or for individual activity.
Power distance	How far an organisation encourages responsibility by learners for their learning or dependence on teachers.
	The degree to which deference to the teacher or engagement with the teacher is expected.
Uncertainty avoidance	The degree to which organisations encourage risk taking, openness and vulnerability, or encourage compliance in learning.
Status-relationships	How far organisations value performance in tests over effective learning practices.
Long-term – short-term orientation	The degree to which the institution values dispositions such as perseverance, persistence over protection of 'face' and respect for established authorities.

The implications of these dimensions can be seen in a number of aspects of classroom learning such as: the structure and length of lessons; the balance of oral and written work; pedagogical language; teachers' questions; learning tasks; the balance of emphasis on subject matter and affective or behavioural issues; the manner in which teaching messages are conveyed; the view of knowledge (Alexander, 1999).

Concluding Thoughts

In this chapter we have explored important 'big picture' ideas about effective learning: people's different conceptions of learning, the influence of context on these, major models of learning, and so on. These will stay with us throughout the book. We have also started to clarify effective learning and begun to examine how it may be promoted in classrooms – through activity, collaboration, responsibility and meta-learning (see Table 2.2).

But is that what we see in classrooms? And how are we looking at classrooms? We now turn in Chapter 3 to address these questions in detail. Then in Chapter 4 we examine influences that can work against the promotion of effective learning in schools and classrooms. And in Chapter 5 we consider teachers who have created conditions where effective learning flourishes, despite these constraints.

What Do We See in Classrooms? – Ways of Seeing

In this chapter
The need for a better way of looking
The shift to focus on the classroom
Learners' views of the classroom and learning
Different views of learning – different ways of seeing

The point of this chapter is to consider our ways of looking at classrooms – and to consider more than the traditional or dominant approach. This is important for two reasons:

- In 'changing the script' of classrooms toward something which better promotes effective learning, we can help ourselves by knowing in detail how we want the classroom to look. This is not because we are putting on some sort of 'show', but because it will give more detail to the professional vision which guides us in our improvements.
- The dominant and usually unexamined approaches to looking at classrooms can act as a negative force against improvement, because they are inadequate for examining learning. We need to understand this, and be able to challenge it constructively.

The Need for a Better Way of Looking

Teachers themselves can fall into looking at classrooms in ways which are unexamined. An illustration of this occurs when asking teachers to view a video of a classroom lesson and giving them no particular framework for doing so. When asked to comment on what they saw a very high proportion of those comments (often 75 per cent and sometimes more) will do two things: focus on the teacher, and focus on the negative. In adopting this way of seeing, sometimes called the 'stance of the hostile witness', teachers have unintentionally turned themselves into some sort of judge or inspector rather than acting as a professional observer of the scene. When this phenomenon is made clear following the video discussion, some of the teacher-colleagues express annoyance and suggest they have been tricked: this is certainly not the intention, but the point here is to illustrate how the prevalent and unexamined ways of looking at classrooms can trick all of us into seeing too little.

These ways of looking have three effects which we find teachers themselves also recognise:

1 *Professional defensiveness* Even with colleagues who come to join a lesson, teachers often feel defensive because they sense that the spotlight is on them, rather than on the activities, the learning, and so on. So peer observation can become tinged with the same dynamics as when an inspector calls:

> There must be few teachers who can remain entirely indifferent to the presence of strangers in their classroom. Indeed when the visitor is one of Her Majesty's Inspectors the reaction of the inspected is apt to betray the most violent distaste, whether disguised or not beneath a layer of diplomatic affability in the presence of the scrutineer. (A Correspondent, *The Times*, 31 March, 1959: 10)

Do you recognise this sort of response when an inspector calls? One part of the response is the language of 'strangers' and of a teacher's 'possession' of the classroom. But we do not attribute this to individual defensiveness: it is something more widespread about teaching as a profession. We understand it more when we remember that teaching is a profession which is often in the public eye, for which the goals and methods are always contested, and schools are complex busy places. But such defensiveness is not the best ingredient for learning, including teachers' learning.

2 *Missing the point about classroom learning* The focus on observing teachers and their performance in the classroom displays the ancient view of teachers as deliverers and leaves students passive – sometimes not even a focus of viewing at all. This too may be a reflection of some key issues, such as the fact that learning itself is not fully visible, so there will always be limitations for an observer. But we do need to find the frameworks to help us focus on the observable things in a classroom which are associated with learning.

3 *A mechanical focus on the teacher-centred classroom* Especially in a context where there is a public and powerful pressure on performance, where policies distort the responsibility for learning and achievement and the discourse changes to one which colludes with a focus on the teacher and a focus on the negative (see the next chapter). In the UK the government rhetoric of 'raising standards' has

the effect of changing the discourse so that observers focus on teachers' performance in narrow ways which do not embrace the complexity of teaching and learning. Neither does it embrace what is necessary for improvement to occur:

> A public discourse has been established which accounts for successful teaching in mechanistic and superficial terms as a set of external behaviours which are not linked to an understanding of learning. It is based on teacher performance, not interaction between teachers and learners. (Wrigley, 2000: 24)

Examples of the ways of seeing classroom events in mechanical terms include such ideas as 'time on task': this is a meaning-free measure of activity, which clearly does not address anything important about what the task is, what it may or may not invite from learners, and so on.

The Shift to Focus on the Classroom

To improve what we see in classrooms, one step is to detach our gaze from the teacher and look at the wider scene – the scene which has such a powerful effect on both teachers and pupils. As the classroom is such a complex environment, there are many ways to achieve a wider focus, even if some of them may feel unfamiliar at first. One indicative set of headings (Watkins and Whalley, 1993) might be:

The classroom context and its properties

- Physical setting
- Social environment
- Psychological climate

The educational context of the classroom, its patterns and structures

- Goals
- Tasks
- Social structure
- Timing and pacing
- Resources
- Teacher's role

With such a framework of headings a lot more about how a classroom operates could be examined in some depth. However, even this rich set of investigations could run the risk of missing the point – and the point is learning. When it comes to developing a focus on learning there may be ways in which the many headings in such a framework operate and vary together in sorts of clusters.

An example of looking at different clusters of classrooms was given by Getzels (1977), who proposed four descriptions of classrooms each of which he suggested reflects the view of learning informing it. These are summarised in Table 3.1.

Table 3.1 Images of the classroom and visions of the learner (after Getzels, 1977)

Image of the Classroom	Vision of the learner	Associated ideas
Rectangular	Empty learner	Learning when specific responses were connected with specific stimuli through the mediation of pleasure or pain. Organism would do nothing to learn or think if it were not impelled to such activity by primary drives like hunger or thirst or by externally applied motives like reward and punishment. Stimulus and the response were believed to be determined by the teacher. Hence their place in front of classroom, sometimes on a platform, and pupils placed so that they would not turn away from the only source of the learning experience: the teacher.
Square	Active learner	Learners see discrete stimuli as 'belonging together' as making a configuration or a Gestalt. Learning was conceived of not only as a connective process but as a dynamic cognitive and affective process as well. From this point of view the learner – not the teacher – became the centre of the learning process.
Circular	Social learner	Learning was perceived as occurring through interpersonal actions and reactions, each person in the classroom serving as a stimulus for every other person. A circular or group-centred classroom where everyone faces everyone else is the most sensible and practical, even necessary, learning environment.
Open	Stimulus-seeking learner	Learning, thinking, problem-solving and intellectual exploration may also be ends in themselves, as the organism seeks to *increase* as well as decrease stimulation … The central fact in the growth and development of children is … the opportunity for effective interaction with the environment, as manifested in the child's curiosity and exploratory activity. The learner is a problem-finding and stimulus-seeking organism … innately curious and will explore without adult intervention; exploratory behaviour is self-perpetuating.

Crucially, Getzels points out that some classroom environments which at first glance would lead many to judge them as chaotic, when viewed with a more discerning way of seeing, can be seen to be achieving a lot.

To view the open classroom 'as appearing haphazard and looking like a playroom but not like a classroom' … is so only when I regard the arrangements in light of the traditional vision of the learner. If I now regard these arrangements with a vision of the learner as a stimulus-seeking organism, what did not look like a classroom looks very much like an appropriate place for children to learn … Now it is the more familiar traditional classroom of sterile spaces and bare walls, straight rows and rigid chairs, that does not look like a classroom and seems an inappropriate place for learning. (Getzels, 1977: 16)

It would be a hazard to use Getzels' work in such a way that it became a typology merely to categorise different classrooms by their organisational form. Rather, we need to examine in further detail what aspects of a classroom might be brought into focus by different ways of viewing learning.

Since pupils may spend time focusing on their classrooms and on learning, learners' views may provide a further source of illumination on this issue, and the need to move on from traditional views of classrooms. But what do learners see in classrooms?

Learners' Views of the Classroom and Learning

What children see in classrooms has an influence on the way they understand learning, and especially learning in school. One powerful and interesting way to explore these understandings is to ask them to draw or take photographs of learning.

In producing these images children do not simply represent what they see, but they do make use of three resources: the cultural images of classrooms, teachers and schools (such as sums, whiteboards, alphabets); the experiences of schools, teachers and classrooms and especially what they see; and their individual drawing preferences. The production of images always requires young people to make choices about what to include, or to omit, how to frame their image, about the relationships between elements of their images. When asked to draw a process such as learning, as opposed to a teacher or a good learner, the children's choices and decisions are especially significant.

In looking at children's drawings there is much diversity in the composition and in the separate elements that are included. While we may take much pleasure in their drawings, we must not romanticise them as revealing permanent truths; rather we should be mindful that they can contribute to developing understandings of learning for both teachers and learners. The examples that follow illustrate some of the themes that are evident in children's drawings.

In Chapter 2 we described three models of learning: reception, construction and co-construction, and considered children's drawings that reflected those three models. In a study called 'Regarding Learning', 23 children in a class of six year-olds at Five Elms School, Barking and Dagenham, were asked to draw learning in the classroom (Lodge, forthcoming). We will now discuss two drawings from that collection to illustrate different themes.

Stacey's drawing (Figure 3.1) includes many aspects of the reception view of learning. The key figure is the teacher. Another important feature of the drawing is the five children, each one at a separate desk, and each has paper with writing on before them, representing learning activities as individual, isolated and separate. Stacey drew the desks this way despite the actual arrangement in the classroom in which she was drawing; in reality two children sat at each desk and these were arranged in a tight horseshoe arrangement with no gaps between them.

Stacey has followed two patterns, also noted by Weber and Mitchell (1995) in the USA, by showing the teacher as smiling and standing, and by including sums on the whiteboard. The sums may represent the more abstract learning that children experience in schools, unlike learning outside school. Both the sums and the dominant teacher are features of young people's drawings from a study in three London schools (Harris, 2002), referred to in the previous chapter. These images recur frequently when young people show what they see as learning.

Figure 3.1 Stacey's drawing of learning in the classroom

In Ella's drawing (Figure 3.2) the focus is herself. She is sitting at a single table, with no classmates and no teacher. Her fellow pupils are represented in the pictures behind her on the wall, named as Paige, Ben, Chloe and Dani, as well as a picture of herself. When discussing her drawing about two months after it was completed, Ella said she wanted to include her friends through the displays and that she might add one or two more people if she were to change it. She has referred to undesirable behaviour in some rules provided by Ross and Jamie. She has included details of the equipment found on each table (paper, pencils in pots) as well as the birthday cakes, which had names and dates on them. An interesting addition here is the clock. In contrast to many other drawings Ella has not included the teacher. Her view of learning has many contrasts to Stacey's, despite them being in the same class and sharing the same learning activities.

Figure 3.2 Ella's drawing of learning in the classroom

The 23 drawings depicted learning in relation to their teacher in two ways: dependent upon the teacher (a reception view), with no teacher and the learner as the centre of their own learning (see Ella's picture) which is more akin to the idea of individual sense making, or the construction model. As we might expect, about half of the children represented the teacher as central to their learning, usually with a smiley face. These children may be drawing on the model of 'Learning = being taught', described as the reception model in Chapter 2.

Social relationships are evident in these drawings. Unlike Stacey's individual and separate children, or Ella's focus on herself, many children include their classmates, or like Ella represent each other's presence by including pictures on the wall, each annotated with the name of a friend. Again the children were making deliberate choices, for the pictures on the wall in their classroom that day were not the ones shown in their drawings. These representations indicate an understanding that others can be important in one's learning, but not the co-constructivist idea of building knowledge with others.

In this class a connection between learning and behaviour was included in several drawings. This was done in a number of ways; for example by adding displays of rules, and a *good* and *bad* list of names on the whiteboard (the *good* list included the artist and her friends). One picture was divided down the middle and contrasted right and wrong behaviour in the classroom. Another study noted how talk in the classroom by teachers and young people often blurs the differences between behaviour and learning, and suggests that behaviour is often emphasised over learning in the classroom (Duffield et al., 2000).

The young people in the Regarding Learning project were also given cameras along with the instruction to take photographs connected to learning over several weeks. The class teacher reported that this produced much discussion and questioning among the pupils about why photographs should be taken. Some of the themes mentioned above were reflected in the 113 photographs they took: 21 per cent showed the children in the class engaged in individual seatwork. Another 11 per cent showed workbooks. In other words, about a third of their photographs showed individual tasks associated with writing in books. Only 18 per cent of the pictures included the teacher, and while many of those could be said not to be of her precisely, she was in the picture.

Young children also show awareness of contrasts between different learning experiences, as the next examples illustrate. Emma Brown, from Shears Green Junior School in Gravesend, Kent, asked her class of 8 year-olds to draw two pictures to show the contrast between their learning when the lessons were framed by the TASC (Thinking Actively in a Social Context) wheel (Wallace et al., 2004) and other lessons when this was not the case. The wheel is a planning device which highlights a series of explicit processes that encourage collaboration, responsibility and awareness of learning. Many of the pictures showed contrasts in a number of aspects of the classroom activities:

TASC wheel lessons	*Contrasting classroom lessons*
Students are active	Students are passive
Children are standing	Children are sitting
Young people dominate	Teacher dominates
More children	Fewer children
Teacher is absent	Teacher is central
Children take responsibility	Children don't understand
Children collaborate	Children are isolated
Children display joint products	Children use workbooks
More everyday speech	Commands and requests

The drawings of the TASC wheel lessons show more active learning, sometimes with more responsibility taken by the learner, and much more collaboration. The dominant themes of the other lessons appear to be of a more passive, isolated and teacher-centred experience.

Figure 3.3 Child's drawing of contrasting classrooms (i)

The first pair of these contrasting drawings (Figure 3.3) shows many of the features listed above. In the drawing of the History TASC wheel lesson the young people are taking responsibility ("What shall we do next?", "Shall we cut this out?"). They have a range of materials on the table, and they stand in the central space of the classroom. The TASC wheel is displayed on a wall to one side together with a table and chair, which are neatly tucked away. In the contrasting English lesson only one child is shown, also neatly tucked away at the table with her back to the viewer. The only resources depicted are the book in front of her and the white board on which it displays the date and 'Story'. There is much blank space in the drawing of this lesson.

Figure 3.4 Child's drawing of contrasting classrooms (ii)

The second pair of drawings (Figure 3.4) highlights other differences. Two children are presenting their poster of Tudor clothes, including Ellesha who is 'reading out her comments'. The poster is bigger than either of the children. The other lesson appears to be maths, where Miss Brown is demonstrating 2D shapes on the whiteboard. Four class members are shown, but all we can see is the back of their heads and an indication of their names.

Figure 3.5 Child's drawing of contrasting classrooms (iii)

The third pair of pictures in this set (Figure 3.5) shows three children's very large faces as they present their history project on Tudor homes, with their arms raised and pointing. The other classroom lesson shows maths where the children are telling Miss Brown that they don't understand. They are sitting down at desks with all their equipment in front of them, but their arms and hands are inactive or at least remain hidden.

These three drawings, and the others produced by this class, show clearly that the children understand that learning experiences can vary, and that they can indicate some important features about the variety, and can show how their responses to these experiences can also differ.

The production of drawings and photographs by young people provides an opportunity for them to reflect on their view of learning, as they make choices and decisions about what to include, what to give prominence to and what sources to draw on. Adults looking at what children present as their view of learning are given access to understanding more about learners' understandings and perspectives. The drawings and photographs described here gave the young people and their teachers valuable opportunities to engage in talking about learning.

So how do adults look at classrooms and learning in classrooms? Do they have different frameworks available to them for this purpose?

Different Views of Learning – Different Ways of Seeing

As we try to forge a better way of seeing in the classroom, one which reflects more of our pupils' perceptions and more of our appreciative enquiries around what makes the best learning, we may need to return to the opening point of this chapter and develop better frameworks for viewing classrooms. It may be worth starting with the dominant model, just to emphasise what a thin view of learning it represents. As with Getzels' rectangular classroom and the empty learner, the 'transmission' model which so readily crops up in unexamined talk about learning offers no role for an active learner. As we discussed in Chapter 2, the focus is on the teacher: students' roles are to respond to teaching:

The 'transmission' model: 'Learning = being taught'

Teachers show good command of subjects
Teachers plan effectively
Teachers have clear learning objectives
Teachers interest pupils
Teachers make effective use of time
Students acquire new knowledge or skills in their work
Students show positive responses to teaching
Students show engagement and concentration, and are productive
Teachers assess pupils' work thoroughly and constructively
Teachers use assessment to inform their planning and target-setting
Students understand how well they are doing and how they can improve
(abbreviated from Ofsted, 2003)

The effect of the use of this sort of framework is revealing: a quarter of teachers plan to deliver a more 'formal didactic' lesson than normal during Ofsted inspections (Brimblecombe et al.,1996). But the contradictions of such a scheme are displayed through the feedback which a teacher can receive: 'One of my lessons was marked unsatisfactory due to the lack of co-operation from the pupils although my teaching was considered satisfactory' (Chapman, 2001: 65). So in this model 'good' teaching can continue despite disengagement by pupils!

Shifting the focus towards learning involves attending to what pupils are doing, and especially what they need to do in order to be active learners and creators of meaning. A framework for observing in this way derives from a constructivist approach, as discussed in the previous chapter:

The 'construction model': 'Learning = individual sense-making'

> Students are engaged in active participation, exploration and research
>
> Students are engaged in activities to develop understanding and create personal meaning through reflection
>
> Student work shows evidence of conceptual understanding, not just recall
>
> Students apply knowledge in real world contexts
>
> Students are presented with a challenging curriculum designed to develop depth of understanding
>
> Teacher uses diverse experiences of students to build effective learning
>
> Students are asked by the teacher to think about how they learn, explain how they solve problems, think about their difficulties in learning, think about how they could become better learners, try new ways of learning (Thomas, 2003)
>
> Assessment tasks are performances of understanding, based on higher order thinking
>
> (abbreviated from Brown and Fouts, 2003)

Viewing a classroom with this sort of framework will draw very different phenomena to the observer's attention. It may also highlight again the current state of classrooms. It is of interest to note the findings from one study using this framework to observe a total of 669 classrooms, from 34 schools, over a four month period of time in the western USA:

> The general findings of this study were that strong constructivist teaching was observable in about 17% of the classroom lessons. The other 83% of the lessons observed may have contained some elements of constructivist teaching, but as many as one-half of the lessons observed had very little or no elements of constructivist teaching present. (Abbott and Fouts, 2003: 6–7)

Do you think a similar pattern might prevail in your context? Again it is of interest to note that the same study gave evidence of 'large positive correlations between constructivist teaching and student achievement' (2003: 5).

But the distribution of the more constructivist classrooms was not even: it was biased more towards classes of children of higher income. Teachers may activate these more effective views of learning for particular groups of pupils, based on some idea of what is appropriate for that group. So teachers' beliefs about who can learn in what way are brought to our attention.

A further step in our ways of seeing classrooms becomes possible when we note that the constructivist framework above broadly focuses on learners as individuals. Some of the wider issues of the classroom, such as its climate and social arrangements, are not explicitly addressed. It is possible and indeed important to do so, not least because teachers themselves have an understanding and an ambition on such matters which are not supported through the dominant discourse about classrooms.

If you ask a group of teachers to say what they want classroom life to be like in their classrooms they will mention many things about social relations, peer helping, the intellectual climate and so on. These are some of the features of a classroom as a learning community which regularly arise in teachers' hopes and ambitions, despite the fact that the dominant way of seeing learning is silent about such matters. After one such discussion in a group of teachers, Ruth, who had been teaching in the UK for five years, said "I'm amazed at this discussion because it has identified many things which are important to me, but I have not talked about them in the last five years."

A framework for viewing classrooms in this way is offered below, and indicates how the social relations and learning relations are brought together in such a view of classroom learning.

The 'co-construction' model: 'Learning = creating knowledge with others'

Students operate together to improve knowledge

Students help each other learn through dialogue

Learning goals emerge and develop during enquiry

Students create products for each other and for others

Students access resources outside the class community

Students review how best the community supports learning

Students show understanding of how group processes promote their learning

The classroom social structures promote interdependence

Students display communal responsibility including in the governance of the classroom

Assessment tasks are community products which demonstrate increased complexity and a rich web of ideas

(from Watkins, 2005)

Perhaps as a final reminder of how much the dominant way of seeing classrooms unwittingly drives teachers' perceptions of the classroom, it is worth mentioning a recent event. A group of teachers who were just completing a course in conjunction with their local university were offered a chance to examine ideas about classrooms as learning communities, along the lines of this last framework above. As a stimulus to discussion they were given four photographs of classrooms which could contain such elements, collected from the 1890s to the 1980s. Some of the participants were very vocal at how thought-provoking the brief session had been, and powerfully commented "I had no idea that classrooms could be like that."

But there are indeed rich and connected examples of classrooms which foster learning effectively: the point is that they are perhaps in a minority and are not well supported by the dominant way of seeing. So let us now examine further what seems to maintain that dominant view.

CHAPTER 4

Faster Learning, Better Teaching, More Testing, Higher Scores: The Big Picture and its Effects on Learning in Classrooms

In this chapter
The effects of testing and the emphasis on test performance
Defensive teaching
Learning in the performance context
A focus on teaching not learning
Grouping by 'ability'
Curriculum distortions
Target setting
Three more distractions from learning
Concluding thoughts: tensions for teachers

We now examine some current factors in the context beyond the school, and how they typically influence learning and teaching in classrooms. These factors come from a wide range of sources: institutions, government agencies, a range of people with different priorities and expectations. We consider how these external voices mix with voices within the school and within the classroom to influence the activities of teaching and learning.

Whose are these voices? We suggest the loudest voices belong to media, government, their agencies (for example, in England the National College of School Leadership, QCA, Ofsted) and local government. It may seem that these official voices operate for control and compliance. For example, their themes include assessment and performance in tests, accountability, new initiatives and strategies, talk about 'ability', curriculum 'delivery' and targets. Other voices such as those of parents, unions, subject associations, consultants, researchers may also be articulating concerns which reflect their interests. Some voices, especially the official ones, have more influence than others. They achieve this through powerful judgements and direct consequences for teachers (for example in their level of pay) and for schools (being 'named and shamed'). This creates a climate of increased fear. The least influential voices are often those of teachers and young people.

These voices often make statements about teaching and learning, but they are rarely based on comprehensive evidence, more on persistent folk theories about learning and teaching. Bruner (1996) has described 'folk theories' about pedagogy which are embedded in our culture. One of the most common beliefs is that of teaching by showing (for example apprenticeship), which implies that you learn by watching. A second and connected belief is that of teaching as telling, which implies that learning is listening. This is common in policy assumptions, designs of national curricula and so on. Less common are the beliefs in children as thinkers and children as knowledgeable. Alongside the folk views of pedagogy we also find folk views of learners, such as them having fixed 'abilities'. Those who have researched these matters in detail highlight the destructive effects of the use of 'crude, oversimplifying and debilitating constructs of ability in teaching' (Hart et al., 2004).

In this chapter we examine how the combination of these influences impacts on teaching and learning in classrooms, especially when they are overlaid with fears about the consequences. These fears often distort content, devalue some aspects of effective learning and diminish the experience of learning for many young people. We consider teaching, learning, pupil grouping, and the curriculum, and then identify fads that are responses to this climate. We explore what can happen to learning in a climate where the teacher takes control of learning in the classroom, noticing that it can encourage passivity in learners, a curriculum that has little connection to their lives, minimal collaboration, and no time allowed for young people to consider how they learn.

Policy-makers have for many years of school reform acted as though 'fixing' teachers would produce good learning. The focus of many reforms has been on closer and closer definitions of what it means to be a good teacher, the competencies of good teaching and prescribing both the content of the teaching and the overall strategies, making schemes 'teacher proof'. This has led to teachers feeling that they are not able to be creative or respond to the needs of learners and has diminished their sense of professionalism (Moore, 2004). Levin points out that educational reform also treats pupils in a similar fashion:

> The history of education reform is a history of doing things to other people, supposedly for their own good … Even though all the participants in education will say that schools exist *for* students, students are still treated almost entirely as objects of reform (2000: 155, emphasis in original).

The Effects of Testing and the Emphasis on Test Performance

In order to give added urgency and importance to transforming teaching, the 'outcomes' of teaching have been increasingly emphasised, but in a very particular way – outcomes in terms of young people's performance in tests. The most significant aspect of recent reforms in England has been testing. There is a vast industry of testing and classifying children today (Alderson, 2003: 25), despite the fact that the reliability of tests means that up to one third of children's gradings are wrong (Wiliam, 2001; Black, 2005). When current tests are used for selection at 11 years 'the candidate ranking system has the potential to misclassify up to two-thirds of the test-taking cohort by as many as three grades' (Gardner and Cowan, 2005: 145), and when used for in-school guidance the questionable reliability of national assessment data in respect of the performance of individual children offers little predictive validity (Doyle and Godfrey, 2005).

Pupils in schools in England are subjected to more national assessments than in any other country in the world (Richards, 2000). Today young people are tested and assessed more often than in any previous period. There are also 'optional' tests produced by the National Assessment Agency (formerly a part of the Qualifications and Curriculum Authority) for Years 3, 4, 5, 7 and 8 and 'progress' tests for Year 7 pupils who are on the borderline between attainment levels. Practice tests are also included in young people's school experiences, the majority of young people seeing these 'extra' tests as 'useless', 'irritating' and 'time-wasting' (Carnell, 2004). The emphasis on test results and performance, rather than on learning, reinforces a view that only experiences to enhance test performance are important.

To illustrate the way in which this emphasis on testing and performance is affecting teaching and learning we include an example of one teacher's struggle to maintain rich learning experiences in his classroom in the face of pressure for performance. Then we analyse the influences of pressure for performance on teaching.

'Stand and Deliver': John Sullivan

What happens to teachers near examination time? We cram. We stand and deliver. We teach students to jump through hoops whose dimensions we have not set. Resultant pedagogies lead to crude *ventriloquy*: students learn to be operated by academic discourses rather than operating them.

As an illustration, here is the story of a recent Monday.

During Lesson One, I ask five 13 year-olds to write a hierarchical Person Specification for their ideal teacher. Unanimously voted Quality Number One is *someone who listens.* Number Two is *someone who explains clearly.* Number Three is *someone who allows us our own opinions.* It is a heartening start to the week. I make silent vows.

I then spend Lesson Two with a low ability class finishing coursework for their imminent GCSE examination in English. I ask them what they think of *Macbeth* and assume the listening position. They ask me to tell them what to think so that they can write it down and hand it back to me. The votive candles splutter.

Lesson Three is a meeting with the Head teacher. I have just submitted targets for the department's end of Key Stage Three external assessments. We appear to have committed ourselves to a three per cent increase on last year's results with an arguably weaker cohort. I leave his office and march down the corridor calculating how many lessons we have left with that year group before the examinations.

Lesson Four is with that very year group. I pinch their noses and ladle the content into them. Restlessly they copy yet another examination mantra from the board. One of them asks me "When are we going to *do* something?" By and large, they indulge my panic. I have a growing sensation that I am selling them short.

Why was it is so difficult for me to adhere to the vows of Lesson One? That is how I want to teach: I know it is the best way. Yet what I want to do, or can do, or think is best becomes subordinate to doing what I'm told. The stories I tell myself about my teaching are edited out under pressure from the stories I'm told about *delivery.* (Sullivan, 2000: 79–80)

John Sullivan's account demonstrates that under assessment pressure he takes a 'stand and deliver' position in the classroom adopting the transmission model of teaching (see Chapter 2). The young people respond similarly by depending on the teacher to deliver.

In this example both teacher and learners are affected. The young people have indicated that they want the teacher to listen, explain and be open to their opinions, but as the day progresses teacher and learners find the pressure of targets, coursework and examinations takes priority. The young people demand to be told what to think and write and John reverts to delivery. The pressure from outside has subverted his best intentions.

Pressure from examinations often brings teachers a feeling of responsibility to 'cover the content' of the curriculum. Indeed some people talk about the curriculum as if it were only the subject content. This often results in teachers focusing on their own coverage (not young people's experience of the curriculum), at a fast pace for lessons – highly structured lessons in several parts and a focus on teaching rather than on learning. Lesson objectives are decided in advance by the teacher or framed by the 'scheme of work'.

Here too students feel the impact. A recent review of research (Harlen and

Deakin-Crick, 2002), which adopted the most stringent criteria for admitting evidence, concluded that assessment for summative purposes 'hinders rather than supports the learning of some, and in some cases, all, students'. Negative effects include:

- A lowering of the self-esteem of the less successful students, which can reduce their effort and image of themselves as learners
- A shift towards performance goals rather than learning goals, which is associated with less active and less deep learning strategies and with interest in achievement *per se* rather than interest in the subject
- The creation of test anxiety, which differentially affects students
- Judgements of value being made about students, by themselves and others, on the basis of achievement in tests rather than their wider personal attainment
- The restriction of their learning opportunities by teaching which is focused on what is tested and by teaching methods which favour particular approaches to learning (Harlen and Deakin-Crick, 2002: 60).

In their own words, some 12 year-old students describe the negative influence of testing on learning:

> "I don't think testing is that good because sometimes people crack under the pressure and get nervous. Coursework is better."
> "I don't like them [tests] but I think you need them because they tell how you are getting on in school life and what you need to do to improve it. It doesn't help me enough because you don't know what you have done right or wrong anyway."
> (Carnell, 2004)

As we shall see in more detail in later chapters (8 and 10) this dominant response to testing is not the only response.

Defensive Teaching

When pressure on the teacher includes their accountability for test results, we notice that many teachers adopt 'defensive teaching' (McNeil, 1988). Attention to managing pupils increases and attention to learning goals decreases. Young people's behaviour dominates teachers' thinking, and fear of the children being 'out of the teachers' control', can result.

In classrooms it is often the teacher who:

- decides the content of lessons
- designs and decides the activities through which the young people will learn
- controls the pace at which activities are undertaken
- controls and regulates the flow of communications in the classroom (who gets to speak, for how long, and about what)

- decides how the learning will be assessed, often within the school or external context
- evaluates the quality of learning often within the school or external context (Weimer, 2002).

It is common for teachers to respond to the external pressures and voices by increasingly controlling the classroom experience (Deci et al., 1982; Flink et al., 1990). McNeil observed teachers who imposed control by fragmenting, simplifying or omitting complex aspects of what was to be learned. The knowledge was presented in what was believed to be more digestible forms. Note the metaphors that emphasise absorption or consumption as in the transmission model (see Chapter 2). For example, as the test approaches the content of what is to be learned is reduced to lists or outlines, reducing the information to its simplest forms.

At its most mechanical the three or four part lesson has been promoted by national strategies. It bears marked similarity to the five part lesson of Johann Friedrich Herbart (1776–1841). Some recognition of the dangers of this strategy becoming mechanistic, and of dividing every lesson this way, is perhaps reflected in the change of name to 'the structured lesson' (Stobart and Stoll, 2005).

Fragmentation and simplification limit the complexity of the learning process. The effect can be that issues cease to be controversial by collapsing opposing opinions into mere repetition of a settled story. For example, in a sex education programme HIV/AIDS was presented as a list of ways in which transmission of the infection occurs, with the associated 'do's and don'ts' of safer sex (Carnell, 1999). There was no emotional or interpersonal consideration. The school was worried about handling controversy and parents' complaints, although when asked parents did not raise any objections.

The outcome of fragmentation and simplification is mystification (McNeil, 1988). Such approaches do not encourage participation in dialogue and participatory activities. The engagement is simplified, unemotional and non-controversial. This discourages effective learning by denying the emotional and the participatory aspects. Certainties in such a controlled situation can be experienced as attractive by students, as John Sullivan described above. "They ask me to tell them what to think so that they can write it down and hand it back to me." But John also noticed that both they and he became uneasy as they asked "When are we going to *do* something?" "By and large, they indulge my panic. I have a growing sensation that I am selling them short."

There are other dissatisfactions: bite-size activities deny young people opportunities to experience making slow progress on complicated tasks and to find the pleasure in cumulative progress. They are also denied opportunities to develop resilience (Claxton, 1999). Exceptions to this trend make the point: after a creativity week of sustained activities on a single theme, a primary school pupil told her teacher how nice it was to really get into the topic and to complete it for once.

The pressure to produce 'evidence' of learning promotes the view of learning as 'work', mainly as the production of a written outcome. In one primary school, the teachers found that the children did not believe they had learned properly until they had 'written it down'. Many teachers are familiar with the view expressed by young people that a lesson without writing is a lesson without work. One young person thought that writing enabled her learning: 'If you concentrate a lot and do lots of writing your handwriting gets better and you are collecting stuff inside your brain' (quoted in Carnell, 2004). This is a good example of what Freire (1970) describes as the 'banking' conception of education where knowledge is deposited. This is a limited view of learning – basically memorisation – which is not the kind of learning that helps young people in the twenty first century (Watkins et al., 2002).

A further feature of defensive teaching is the dominance of the idea of pace – usually a brisk and relentless pace. Accelerating the pace of a lesson means that some of the more deliberative activities in learning are seen as inefficient, such as discussion, discovery, sharing knowledge and reviewing strategies. The purpose of the emphasis on pace is supposedly to ensure coverage of the curriculum and to move young people on, not because they are ready but because they will fall behind the plan. It focuses on the teacher's agenda rather than young people's and is unlikely to promote effective learning.

Learning in the Performance Context

The emphasis on assessment and testing, and young people's performance in tests, promotes a belief that performance is what learning in the classroom is all about. But the relation between learning and performance is not simple, and better performance is not achieved by merely emphasising performance.

A better understanding of the dynamics of learning and performance can be achieved by considering how learners orient themselves to learning. Such beliefs have a very powerful influence on how they go about their learning. Dweck (1999), throughout decades of research with children and adults, suggests that people can respond to learning tasks in a range of ways which lie along the dimension summarised in Table 4.1. Sometimes they have beliefs which support a mastery orientation to learning: this means they have a love of learning, seek challenges, value effort and persist in the face of obstacles. We call this a *learning* orientation. On different occasions other beliefs prevent them from improving their learning, especially in challenging situations because they link lack of success to lack of ability. We call this a *performance* orientation.

Table 4.1 Learning and performance orientations (from Watkins et al., 2002, based on Dweck)

Learning orientation	Performance orientation
Belief that effort leads to success	Belief that ability leads to success
Belief in one's ability to improve and learn	Concern to be judged as able, to perform
Preference for challenging tasks	Satisfaction from doing better than others
Satisfaction from success at difficult tasks	Emphasis on competition and public evaluation
Problem-solving and self-instruction when engaged in tasks	Helplessness: negative self-evaluation when task is difficult: "I can't do X"
About improving learning	*About proving what has been learned*

Research which traced the influence of the national curriculum in primary schools (Pollard and Triggs, 2000) led Nias to suggest a worrying trend for young people in primary schools:

> … the structured pursuit of higher standards in English and mathematics may be reducing the ability of many children to see themselves as self-motivating, independent problem-solvers taking an intrinsic pleasure in learning and capable of reflecting on how and why they learn. (2000: xiii)

In the context of these pressures it is a particular irony that the emphasis on performance can depress performance, while a focus on learning can enhance performance.

The focus on testing and improving the performance of young people has led to some practices in classrooms which may or may not promote better test results, but the point is that this is a short-term judgement of schooling. International evidence from secondary schools does not support this trend. A study of 32 countries, with 174,075 fifteen year-old respondents concluded:

> 'Achievement press' which was measured by students' perceptions of the extent to which teachers emphasise academic performance and place high demands on students, is only moderately related to performance, and the effect on performance, on average across OECD countries, on the mathematical and scientific literacy scales is not statistically significant. (OECD, 2001a: 205)

An analysis of evidence on the performance of UK secondary schools (Gray et al., 1999) identified that improving schools have gone through three approaches in the last decade. First, they have adopted new tactics to maximise their showing in the performance tables (enter more pupils, mentor those on the borderline and so on). Second, they have adopted internal strategies to improve their schools (giving more responsibility to pupils, building improvement strategies in particular departments, integrating pastoral and academic responsibilities). Third, a small group of the highest improving schools has shifted beyond these two approaches into an area which builds its capacity to improve, through an overarching focus on learning.

An emphasis on test performance is unlikely to promote effective learning as it does not encourage activity, collaboration and independence from the teacher and does not allow time for learning about learning. Indeed, there is long-standing evidence that it leads to a more controlling form of teaching. Some of the research on this was undertaken over twenty years ago and is worth quoting at length because of the similarities with today's studies:

> In our interviews with teachers, we have heard over and over how many of them have lost some of their enthusiasm for teaching (Deci and Ryan, 1982). Initially excited and motivated to teach, to challenge and motivate the children in their classrooms, they tell of how the external pressures of standardized curricula, competency tests, and other manifestations of a culture obsessed with achievement have robbed them of autonomy and creativity with respect to teaching and had a negative impact on their own interest and effectiveness in the classroom milieu. Their reports of how such factors cause them to be less supportive of the children's autonomy led us to another experiment.
>
> We explored the effects of externally set performance standards on teaching styles (Deci et al., 1982). Two groups of subjects were asked to teach students how to solve spatial-relations problems. Both groups of subjects were given the same instructions, except that, for one group, a sentence was added telling them that, as teachers, it was their responsibility to see to it that their students performed up to standards. While this addition might seem subtle, it led to dramatic effects. The 20-minute teaching session was tape-recorded and later analyzed. It revealed that those teachers in the performance standards condition made three times as many utterances and their utterances were more likely to be directing, controlling, and to include words like 'should' and 'must'. In short, the pressure created by mentioning performance standards led the subjects to be much more controlling in the teaching task. And this of course is ironic, because so much research has suggested that the less controlling the teacher, the more likely it is that the students will perform well. (Ryan et al., 1985: 46)

A Focus on Teaching not Learning

The language of much policy in the UK, and its underpinning rationale, creates a focus on teaching. Examples may be found in the literacy and numeracy strategies, and the Key Stage 3 strategy. For example, if you search DfES documents for sentences which begin 'Successful learning takes place when ...', then what is the next word? Yes, it's 'teachers' (DfES, 2004a).

Recently the idea of 'personalised learning' has been exemplified by the DFES in a similar way, in terms of teaching:

> For teachers, it [personalised learning] means a focus on their repertoire of teaching skills, their subject specialisms and their management of the learning experience. Personalised learning requires a range of whole class, group and individual teaching, learning and ICT strategies to transmit knowledge, to instil key learning skills and to accommodate different paces of learning. (DfES, 2004b: 9)

In research into the Key Stage 3 strategy, one teacher observed that there was more talk about planning and structure and that focusing on planning and objectives has been important for some teachers (Carnell, 2004). But what is being planned? One answer highlights the start of lessons: 'There has been a massive range of engagement activities at the beginning of lessons that has started lessons with a bang and brought them [young people] in more quickly' (p. 45). What is missing here is talk about learning.

This has serious implications for young people's learning. As one teacher put it:

> The language has had an impact on teaching. Teachers are much more open to discussion about their teaching because they are much more confident about what we see as good teaching. This has been excellent. I am not sure if the KS 3 strategy has transformed the learning but it certainly has transformed the teaching so it probably has transformed the learning. (2004: 43)

But, as teachers know, learning cannot be assumed just because teaching has happened. This assumption that transforming teaching transforms learning needs to be challenged, as does the regular use of terms such as 'teaching and learning strategies' and 'teaching and learning policies', in which the real attention paid to learning is minimal.

There are comparable findings from other research projects. For example, Stobart and Stoll (2005) conclude that a more radical approach to the learning of 11 to 14 year-olds is needed. In his (2004) paper 'Still no Pedagogy?' Alexander questions the view that other government strategies have been successful at improving the quality of teaching and raising standards in schools. Quoting a number of research projects he concludes that intended changes to teaching and learning have not yet been fully realised and that it is difficult to draw conclusions about the effects on pupil learning.

Grouping by 'Ability'

Another practice that has become more common in schools and has been recommended by government voices is the grouping of young people into 'ability' sets. The rationale is that it improves performance, but the evidence for this is inconclusive (Ireson and Hallam, 2001). A more recent research review for the DfES concluded with the same point: 'Especially with regard to attainment, studies have not shown evidence that streamed or set classes produce, on average, higher performance than mixed ability classes' (Kutnick et al., 2005: 47). Such grouping decisions are based on considerations about teaching rather than on what facilitates learning most effectively.

This young person highlights the impact of such practice on his feelings and his learning:

> You get put into sets for Maths, English and Science on how the tests went. If you are in the lower set you are disappointed in yourself and I think that all the people in the top set are laughing at us and I feel really bad about myself and that might get in the way of me learning. (Carnell, 2004: 33)

Young people speak about 'top', 'middle' and 'bottom' sets and they have the view that being in the 'top' set means certain privilege, like having the 'best' teachers. Young people have come to understand some of the ideas about being in mixed ability groups that impact on their learning, and that 'if you are all clever then you are not going to be able to help each other', whereas 'slow learners need more help' (Carnell, 2004).

A model of pedagogy based on 'transformability' has been constructed by Hart et al. (2004). This model is based on the view that all young people can become better learners, that children's futures as learners are not pre-determined, and that teachers can help and ultimately transform young people's capacity to learn.

Curriculum Distortions

An over-emphasis on testing and assessment distorts the curriculum. This was captured by an 11 year-old pupil who told his teacher that this year had been 'SATs, SATs, SATs, SATs, and RE' (Daukes, 2004: 13). Another 11 year-old commented on his narrowed curriculum, observing that the 9 and 10 year-old children were doing better than he was at design and technology and art, since "we don't do these".

It also gives the impression to young people that if what is measured is valued, then what is not measured is not valued. Many young people adopt a strategic approach to school and tests, and choose to focus on 'stuff what counts' (Rudduck et al., 1996). From this point of view, a year without national tests (for example Year 8) is seen as 'a free year':

> 'You can be laid back. You don't really have to work.'
> 'It's a rest. You don't get stressed out. No tests.' (Carnell, 2004: 28)

An over-tested and non-responsive curriculum increases the chance that young people see little connection between their lives and what they are learning at school, as recently confirmed in research with 12 year-old students (Carnell, 2004). They saw their learning as 'important for after you leave school' or 'important for the next year'. Even when pressed young people found it difficult to get beyond the view that learning was just for the future and highly instrumental:

> 'You need information for the future because if you don't get a good education you won't get a good job.' (Carnell, 2004: 24)

Some struggled to find connections between the curriculum as they experienced it and the rest of life, but suggested the following could be relevant:

> 'Maths for money and how to spend it.'
> 'Learning a foreign language. You can then speak French or Spanish on holiday.'
> 'Science, first aid in case someone gets hurt.' (2004: 24)

The curriculum is experienced as disconnected from their lives. What has become important is what is to be tested. While some examinations and coursework offer great opportunities for young people to show their knowledge and skills, the content and methods of other tests do not (Alderson, 2003). For example there are few tests that measure skills in collaboration, co-constructive dialogue (learning through conversations) or meta-learning. Yet these are crucial aspects of effective learning.

Target Setting

Individual and cohort target setting was enthusiastically endorsed by the UK government until recently, but still has a place in the official discourse and policy of England. Our view is that relying on the setting of targets is unlikely to help young people learn well. There are several reasons for this. First, the setting of targets is often imposed upon young people (as it has been on teachers too), which does not encourage them to see these targets as their responsibility to achieve.

Second, the setting of targets does not help young people achieve them. It is understanding *how* to improve their learning that they need. In some schools the setting of the target becomes all-important and a valuable opportunity to talk more about learning is lost.

Third, there are the affective aspects of target setting: pressure involved in having targets, and the de-motivating effects of not achieving them. This comment was the response of a Y8 student:

> 'In some ways it is good, in some ways bad. Good because it gives you something to work for but bad because it like gets in the way and there is too much pressure.' (Carnell, 2004: 34)

Some young people went as far as saying targets were counter-productive and limited learning, interfering with their own intentions:

I think it is pointless because if you want to do something then you will do it yourself. If you set targets then you just go for those targets rather than going for an overall. You try and do everything for yourself to do your best, the best you can do in school so you don't need targets because you could do everything to the best of your ability and you don't need targets. (2004: 38)

Fourth, students come to see setting targets as a futile exercise, writing down something that they knew they could already achieve, or writing something for its own sake:

'You don't really follow them. They are just there.'
'They don't help much as you forget. The teacher writes it but you can't read it.'
(2004: 39)

Fifth, other research suggests that although teachers may try to engage young people in talking about targets this does not extend their understanding of learning because the conversation focuses on performance rather than learning. Often the teacher talks in a generalised way, where the student would be more engaged by a narrative form, based on their lived experience of learning. As a result such conversations do not generate understanding about learning (Lodge, 2003).

These responses to target setting underscore the view that a focus on performance may inhibit performance whereas a focus on learning may enhance performance (Watkins, 2001).

Three More Distractions from Learning

In a context which emphasises testing, teaching and targets, it is hardly surprising that there is an impoverished focus on learning. But it is a little surprising that some of the attempts to meet the demands of outside influences use the term 'learning' but do not provide a real focus on it. We see them more as fads or fashions, and here we discuss three: learning styles, brain-based learning and accelerated learning.

Learning styles

The attraction of learning styles is understandable. It reminds teachers that young people learn in different ways, and that activities for learning should be varied. However, many issues arise by focusing on learning styles: learners are viewed as non-changing; matching the teaching with learners' styles is impossible; a thin description of learning results; the focus often remains on teaching rather than learning. Teachers find that using learning styles often results in a dead end. There is a potential trap in focusing on learning styles – it categorises and obscures the significance of the context and that young people need to develop a range of styles for different purposes and different contexts (Lodge, 2003). Young people need to be adaptive learners, so the teacher should encourage development of a full range of learning approaches.

The concept of learning styles is not robust. A major and comprehensive review of research found that many of the methods used to identify individual learning styles were unreliable and that using the idea of matching teaching and learning styles has a negligible impact (Coffield et al., 2004b). It concluded by identifying three key issues: 'labeling, vested interests, and overblown claims' (2004b: 137). The first author more recently described a DfES booklet on learning styles as 'woefully uninformed about research. It is also impractical, patronising, uncritical and potentially dangerous to students' (Coffield, 2005). Another report highlights three problems with using the concept of learning styles. First, the research evidence of using learning styles is highly variable; second, there is usually even less evidence relating to classroom use; third, many teachers use it poorly (Hargreaves, 2004).

Brain-based learning

The term 'brain-based' refers to learning or teaching practices which claim to have their foundation in understanding how the brain operates. MRI scanning techniques help us view some of the complex working of the brain but attempts to use this evidence draw on doubtful metaphors of the machine or computer. MRI scans may help us see electrical activity in the brain, but knowing where activity in the brain takes place when, for example, we read is not adding much to our knowledge of how we learn to read. Other simplifications of the complexity of the brain lead to some strange practices: for example juggling, which claims to support the linkage between left and right sides of the brain, is unnecessary as the brain is constructed to do this anyway. Some programmes promoting brain activity are commercial and 'have no evidence in cognitive neuroscience' (Hargreaves, 2004: 14).

The focus on the brain can suggest that learning only happens in the brain. But learning is not all in the head. Much learning for children involves physical learning, and any sports person, musician or artist can talk about other bodily sites of learning. As the constructivist model in Chapter 2 points out learning is about understanding and sense-making, so it could be said to be in our language and strongly influenced by how we talk to ourselves. And the co-constructivist model would suggest that learning is in dialogue, in relationships and in our culture. All of these are de-emphasised by this particular fad.

Accelerated learning

Accelerated learning is a *pot pouri* of lists, charts and diagrams to help train young people to improve their memory. Its proponents draw on a number of sources including for example learning styles, target setting, mnemonics, multiple intelligences, brain-based learning and brain gym. It is presented in lively and expensive sessions, which often provoke enthusiasm in teachers. However, teachers find that it does not generate much useful practice in their classrooms either because pupils are categorised, or cannot adapt to subjects, or cannot deal with variations and subtleties in learning. We would question why it is important to learn faster anyway.

Concluding Thoughts: Tensions for Teachers

It may be thought that we have drawn rather a gloomy picture of the possible effects on learning of current official voices. In some classrooms we visit the experience of learning is indeed distressing. We take effective learning to be characterised by activity and collaboration, to be learner-driven and to involve learning about learning, whereas in many classrooms young people are sitting down and writing on their own, being given fragmented material to 'put into their heads' which is unconnected to their lives outside the classroom (see also the evidence from the Campaign for Learning, 2006, cited in Chapter 6). They are not provided with opportunities for learning more about their learning as there is always more to cover or more practice for tests. They are becoming dependent upon their teachers, wanting to score well.

But all of this is still only part of the overall picture. We have presented it as a dominant response but it is not the only response. And although we have focused on current times, it is a response which is evidenced in earlier times, and highlights some ongoing issues in classroom life and learning.

We see the current times as having exacerbated some endemic tensions for teachers, and it makes some sense that the dominant response has been to resolve these tensions in the old way – focusing on teaching and tests. But the same tensions can be resolved in other ways, as we shall examine in the chapters which follow. And for the reasons you highlighted in your appreciative inquiry (Chapter 1) and we subsequently highlighted in modern views of learning (Chapter 2), it is important that we do find a better way.

The tensions which teachers described in their work were identified by Marble et al. (2000) in the following:

- Who is responsible for student performance?
- What does it mean to work with other teachers?

- What is happening in the classroom?
- What is the big picture?

For each of the first three tensions, it was possible to sense the polarities which teachers experienced, and these are summarised in Table 4.2.

Table 4.2 Teachers' tensions (following Marble et al., 2000)

1 Responsibility for Performance

Teaching decisions depend on external matters, policies, etc.	Teaching decisions are based on knowledge of students.

⬅➡

Student success is independent of teacher action.	Student success depends on teachers' actions and adjustments to student need.

2 Professional Culture

Teaching is seen as a job to be done based on the application of existing skills.	Teaching is seen as a profession that requires continual growth of skills.

⬅➡

Teaching is a solitary act best done alone in the classroom.	Teaching is a collegial act best done in collaborationwith other teachers and their classrooms.

3 Focus on Learning

Teachers believe that knowledge is transmitted.	Teachers believe that knowledge is constructed.

⬅➡

Teachers deliver content complete to students through presentation and lecture.	Teachers create an environment that encourages students to seek knowledge and find personal meaning in that knowledge.

So current pressures encourage teachers to resolve these tensions towards the left hand side of the table. But evidence of many sorts shows that we achieve more lasting goals and better performance by resolving them to the right hand side.

To do so will not necessarily feel comfortable on all occasions. Shifting from the dominant transmission model of teaching to a richer learning environment will often feel like working against the grain. But some of the reasons for change are well put by Weimer:

> The more structured we make the environment, the more structure the students need.
> The more we decide for students, the more they expect us to decide.
> The more motivation we provide, the less they find within themselves.
> The more responsibility for learning we try to assume, the less they accept on their own.
> The more control we exert, the more restive their response. (2002: 98)

In the next chapters we provide some examples where teachers have found the necessary resources within themselves and their environment to organise their classrooms in ways that are not simply a response to the pressures at work in those classrooms. We consider why and how they went about this. We then go on to examine the frameworks for exploring classroom activities in more detail.

CHAPTER 5

Working Against the Grain

In this chapter
Three examples of working against the grain:
• Creating a jigsaw classroom
• Creating an engaged classroom
• Developing a problem-solving classroom
What these stories can help us learn
Concluding thoughts

In Chapter 4 we suggested that the current climate in the UK is characterised by particular 'external' voices, and that teachers' responses to this climate can result in ineffective learning in classrooms. The emphasis is on 'coverage' of the curriculum, performance and testing of young people, and the performance and accountability of teachers.

In this chapter we present three teachers' stories to illustrate that it is possible to respond in different ways to these pressures. It might appear that these teachers are working against the grain. They have resolved the tensions of teaching with learning in mind. We go on to suggest some of the factors that help teachers to resolve these tensions in learning-centred ways.

Three Examples of Working Against the Grain

Creating a jigsaw classroom

This example is from the experience of a Year 11 history teacher concerned with issues of 'coverage' as his students approached their GCSE history examination. His response is not to 'cover' everything by talking at students, but to use a particular approach to structuring the classroom.

Andrew Nockton: Vyners School

My original use of jigsaw methodology came out of the impossibility I often felt of "covering the content" of KS3 National Curriculum or GCSE/'A'-Level syllabus in the allotted time. Now it is my methodology of choice, as in recent years my sense of that pressure has reduced, while "content coverage" has increased. Large topics can be addressed in a much shorter time than if the teacher spends time on each component part.

To help build a learning community through the use of jigsawing, a topic is required that has a number of component parts that can be understood in isolation without necessarily understanding the whole topic. In history teaching, topics that are best understood chronologically for example would not be appropriate, but a good example would be causation. A big question under consideration could be 'What caused World War Two?' Possible answers include German anger at the Treaty of Versailles, Chamberlain's policy of appeasement, the failure of the League of Nations, the Nazi-Soviet Pact of August 1939, the rise of dictators such as Hitler and Mussolini in the 1930s, and the Great Depression.

I divide the class into the number of component parts of the topic that I would like the pupils to address. In this example there are six. Each group would research their particular 'cause' and produce information for the rest of the class – they become the 'experts' in the particular aspect they are investigating, and also decide how they will convey their knowledge to the others – a handout, role-play, and so on.

The important aspect of 'jigsawing' is that the pupils become expert in the whole jigsaw (topic) and not just expert in their particular piece (cause), but the process ensures that each individual's contribution is crucial to the community understanding. When new groups are formed, containing one member of each 'cause' group, each one communicates what they understand about their cause. At the end, a whole class discussion may be used, or perhaps a joint presentation: for other topics I have used creation of verses for a class song or scenes for a class play.

A summative assessment task must be set which consolidates and confirms the students' understanding of the whole topic. In this example, the big question becomes an essay question and each cause might become a paragraph theme. Students are asked to demonstrate their understanding of the possible causes and to create their own argument, perhaps ranking their paragraphs (causes) in order of importance. Obviously at this time, students choose their own main cause, rather than the one that was 'allocated' to them in the preparatory work.

For me, this technique has a number of very positive attributes. The focus shifts from the teacher to the student. The teacher very much facilitates the learning at all stages, from the organisation of the task to the checking for understanding, but the focus is very much on the students. The element of 'collective responsibility' helps students to produce quality contributions. All student work is judged not only by the teacher but more importantly by their peers. A poor contribution can ultimately let the whole class down. I say as the tasks are set 'the class is relying on you…'. Further, the nature of sharing of the pieces of the jigsaw means that student participation within class and interaction with each other increases dramatically. And again when time is short for revision, jigsawing is an excellent way to constructively address large topics.

The methodology requires participation by all members: together with the building of student confidence in putting forward ideas and respecting others' ideas, it is crucial in developing a learning community. (Watkins, 2005: 125–7)

The jigsaw approach will be explored more fully in Chapter 7. Andrew has analysed this approach identifying the following as especially valuable for the students' learning:

- The focus shifts from the teacher to the student
- The teacher's role is to facilitate
- Collective responsibility
- Students' work judged by peers
- Student participation and interaction increase dramatically
- The process is useful for revision.

Despite anxieties about 'coverage', Andrew did not decide to exercise teacher control over the content, which could lead to an increase in his students' dependence on him. He chose not to speed up his 'delivery', or 'accelerate' the teaching. Instead he structured an activity so that every young person in the class 'covered' the content in such a way that they had responsibility for each other's learning. They were more engaged and as a result he found that he did not need to specifically address the behaviour in the classroom.

A jigsaw classroom builds interdependence and encourages responsibility by the students. They are active in their learning, and required to be involved collaboratively. It is possible that Andrew's approach may assist the students' meta-learning, for example the class could review the process they had been through, but this is not specified.

Creating an engaged classroom

Our second example is from the experience of a Year 6 class teacher concerned with the children's apparent lack of responsibility for their own learning.

Wendy Giles: Shears Green Primary School

My purpose was to encourage a class of year 6 children to collaborate and take responsibility for their learning in their PSHE lessons, through the topic of political parties.

As part of the Political Literacy strand of PSHE, our year 6 children were asked to create a Political Party to stand in our class election. Each party had to produce vote-winning ideas that related to our school, and find the most persuasive ways of promoting these ideas in order to win the election.

In order to fulfil the objectives I split the class into mixed ability groups of about six and simply gave the class the brief that they would have to create a party which had sensible vote winning ideas and present their programme in six weeks time to all year 6 classes. I gave them the minimum necessary information and then allowed the groups to get on with the task without any additional input except to question ideas and concepts as I saw them progressing.

The first session required the most intervention by me as some groups were unable to think of sensible ideas that would engage their audience's attention. By listening to their initial thoughts and questioning the appropriateness of them, all of the groups finally managed to find at least three changes that they believed children in the school would want. This was fairly difficult to do for both the children and myself as I could see some of the groups simply waiting for me to give them ideas, which they could then use and expand. I had to seriously consider my function: I intended to be a supporter of ideas and not the facilitator.

As the weeks progressed it became obvious that the children were highly motivated and enjoyed the freedom that the task allowed. It also became quite competitive with each group trying to make their performance better than the others'. One group decided that they would wear rosettes: the following week I had three groups wearing rosettes (they even wore them during playtime!). One group decided to write a persuasive, catchy song: the following week every group had decided to write a persuasive, catchy song. One group put together a dance routine to go with their song: finally I had three groups with a dance routine! One group even had their parents print t-shirts with their party logo.

The persuasive speeches and posters that the groups produced were probably the best pieces of writing that I had seen from many of the children all year. The lower achieving children seemed less afraid of joining in and participated in the writing tasks whereas they would normally have opted for the drawing/colouring activities. But the most encouraging part was the fact that all of the groups evaluated their own performances and speeches without being prompted and could actually see the benefit of doing so.

This project engaged the children from the very first session. They worked sensibly in groups and managed to challenge themselves without even realizing they were. The children took risks and were not afraid to start something again if it wasn't the best it could possibly be. They were happy to share ideas and work with other groups as long as critical feedback was given. The children were striving to produce their best.

Unusually the groups were quite happy for other groups to use their ideas and expand upon them. They didn't seem worried (as they normally would be) that their ideas were being 'stolen'. However it proved quite a challenge for me, as I had to take a step back and allow the finished product to be a true reflection of the children's work and not play a big part in that cycle.

After talking to the children it seems that they enjoyed the freedom that the task allowed.

I would like to review our current schemes of work within each year group, with the hope of finding elements in each, that would lend themselves to this 'alternative, cross-curricular approach' that would allow our children to make more choices of their own.

Coming out of teacher training in years when cross-curricular planning and teaching seem to have been sidelined by structured numeracy and literacy, the project has shown me that there are many children who do not achieve as much as they could within these tight constraints. With this is mind it would be highly beneficial for other members of our staff (probably those who are new to teaching) to go through this 'Alternative Curriculum' programme.

Wendy adopted an approach which encourages:

- active engagement
- collaboration
- choice
- learner-driven feedback.

The engagement of the children was developed through connecting the content with their lives. The children's enthusiasm appears to have engaged the attention and involvement of parents (although some might have been motivated by competition). We note that at first some of the young people were waiting for the teacher to give them ideas. In Chapter 4 we observed how young people can become dependent on their teachers for the right answers. We would also note that Wendy too has become used to taking on this role, and had to struggle a little to find a new way of facilitating, through questioning.

Wendy pointed out that she was most encouraged by the groups' spontaneous review of their performances and speeches and that they perceived the benefits of doing this. As she reviewed the benefits for herself, Wendy showed her own enthusiasm for taking this experiment further, and for her colleagues to have a similar experience.

Developing a problem-solving classroom

Our third example is from the experience of a class teacher of 6 year-olds concerned with developing the persistence of her class in maths lessons.

Justine Turner: Upton Infants School, Dorset

In our audit of the previous year's SATs mathematics papers we found that children did not show any evidence of how they had reached their answers. We began to suspect that children had insufficient experience of problem-solving and did not have the confidence to tackle a problem by applying a range of strategies.

I tried to challenge the students within a supportive atmosphere. The children had already told us they liked challenge. I tried to encourage STICKABILITY where the children had to keep trying. I also made a determined effort to give the children the learning vocabulary by using the language of learning myself and expecting them to use it.

I taught many more mental and written strategies and encouraged the children to discuss the most appropriate strategies in many different ways. The use of response partners increased to become an everyday part of learning and the children were encouraged to see each other as a resource – a sounding board for ideas. I planned opportunities for the children to talk about how they solved a problem, how they reached an answer and to explain their thinking. I encouraged them to find their own ways of working and made a determined effort not to use work sheets and to have more independence in the use of resources. I also gave praise for the working out, rather than a focus on the answer, and deliberately rewarded the strategy. It was very effective. The project directly affected the improvement in the SATs results of this class (27% achieved level 3 as compared to 16% of the previous year's class). As the teaching strategies and the learning dialogue were regularly discussed at planning meetings within the Y2 team, so the effect was widening across the whole year group.

A discussion with the headteacher also revealed that "children were comfortable with the word learning. Learning oriented responses were not confined to children one would consider to be academically more able. All children made valuable contributions to the discussion. They were able to see the purpose for learning as well as enjoyment. They showed that they enjoyed finding out new information as well as acquiring new skills. They recognised the ways in which their teachers helped them and saw them looking for information. They saw that their teacher was a learner too. They recognised the importance of effort and practice."

We would now like to apply what we have learned in mathematics to a more focused, explicit teaching of strategies in reading using the strategy check idea during guided and shared reading sessions. (Adapted from Reed, 2004)

Justine's account emphasises the value of a focus on talking about strategies and how learning happens, even with a very young class. She identified the following as especially valuable for the students' learning:

- An initial enquiry into the blocks to the children's learning
- Developing the children's language about learning
- Building on what the children already said and did (e.g. challenge and response partners)
- Explicit teaching and encouragement
- Talk with the teachers.

Although partly motivated by a desire to increase the performance scores of the pupils, Justine did not focus on performance, rather on being explicit with the children about what would help them learn. She took an active role in this ("I taught more strategies, I planned opportunities for talk, I encouraged them to find their own ways, I gave praise for working out ..."). Some of this went against the grain, as indicated by her comment about not using work sheets.

Justine's approach encourages responsibility by the students and assists the young people in developing language to talk about learning, their meta-learning and collaboration.

What these Stories Can Help Us Learn

In the current climate teachers experience tensions when they make decisions within their classrooms. Learners and teachers need to handle these tensions and this complexity in learning:

> The beginning of wisdom is the discovery that there exist contradictions of permanent tension with which it is necessary to live and that it is above all not necessary to seek to resolve. (Gorz, quoted in Ball, 1998: 81)

The three case studies demonstrate different ways in which the teachers approach these tensions and the problems these tensions cause. Each of them has drawn upon their professional knowledge about learning and about their students to deal with these tensions, and consequently feel comfortable with their decisions. In terms of the tensions for teachers outlined at the end of the last chapter, the three teachers in our case studies handle them in these ways:

- *Tension of responsibility for performance.* Our three teachers reject the notion of the sole authority of external agencies. They find solutions in their professional knowledge of students as learners. Neither teachers nor young people are passive, both have agency and are the key drivers of their learning.

- *Tension about knowledge and how it is acquired.* The three teachers answered this by focusing on the process of learning. They understand that knowledge is constructed together, and teaching is a matter of creating an environment for this.

When they handle the tensions in a learner-centred way, and cope with the experience of feeling that their practice is 'against the grain', they end up confirmed in their stance.

When they are making these decisions it is often helpful for teachers to have confirmation from others in the school. We note that the support of the head-teacher was prominent in Justine's case.

We would also recognise that all three teachers experienced support for their experiments, either as part of a group of Masters students or in LEA projects exploring learning. In their own way each of these teachers had been thinking about their own experiences of being learners. What the Masters courses and the projects provided were opportunities to reflect on their experiences. This informed their enquiry stance about the small changes that they tried (Cochran-Smith and Lytle, 1993). We have noted elsewhere that such supportive opportunities can be crucial to sustaining new practices (Carnell and Lodge, 2002b).

The struggle with these tensions is often experienced as isolating and resulting in lack of good practice, as described in Chapter 4. So what resources do people call upon when they know it's no good listening to the dominant voices? Often this starts with hearing their own voice as a teacher, as a professional, as someone with a wish to make a difference. When they reclaim this voice, and decide what is best for their local context, teachers often find themselves saying, "I just knew it could be better."

Sometimes this requires identifying the teacher's experience of resistance, of dealing with such voices. Some of this might be found within the school itself. For example in a study of 78 schools, teachers were asked: "Do you ever have to do things that are against the rules in order to do what's best for your students?" In learning-enriched schools 79 per cent answered "Yes"; in learning-impoverished schools 75 per cent answered "No" (Rosenholtz, 1989: 157). Effective learning is not about compliance.

Some teachers find small spaces to make changes; not being heroic, but starting with small but important aspects of the classroom. A small step can produce profound changes. In some respects the shifts are huge because they move the focus on to young people, and change the teacher's and the learners' roles. Such changes feel a challenge and take time to adjust to. After time, rather than feeling that they are 'against the grain', such teachers tell us that their practices become engrained in the new script of their classrooms.

For some teachers it is the evidence of more effective learning – noticing what happens when the changes are made – that supports them in their experiments which go against the grain. In this process they are treating themselves as learners, not performers: they do not take the view that they have all the answers in their repertoire already, and are prepared to be involved in professional enquiry in their classrooms.

Concluding Thoughts

Classrooms are complex places. These case studies show that in promoting a rich learning environment for the twenty first century, classrooms may become even more complex as they encourage the following:

- a shift in responsibility from teachers to young people – learner-driven learning
- a focus on learning and a learning language
- a shift in the teacher's role from a behaviour manager to orchestrating learning
- a shift in the young person's role to being a researcher and learning partner with other learners
- an emphasis on reciprocal teaching and learning
- a view that the territory of the classroom is a shared learning space
- more permeable classroom boundaries.

These strategies encourage richer conceptions of learning and the development of a learning community to support effective learning. The following chapters provide frameworks for exploring classroom activities in more detail, considering in turn active learning, collaboration, learner-driven learning, and learning about learning.

PART II

CLASSROOM PROCESSES FOR PROMOTING EFFECTIVE LEARNING

PART II

CLASSROOM PROCESSES FOR PROMOTING EFFECTIVE LEARNING

Active Learning

In this chapter we aim to clarify the term 'active learning', explain why it is essential for effective learning, examine some of the effects of active learning, and then consider issues in applying active learning more widely in the class-room context.

What does the phrase 'active learning' suggest for you? Is it:

- Pupils running around the classroom?
- Children playing in a sand-pit?
- Chaos and confusion?

Or none of these? Something more like:

- Pupils designing and constructing?
- Learners involved in experiments?
- A class creating a newspaper and inquiring into what its readers think?

There are unhelpful connotations of the term 'active learning' (like many other terms with adjectives associated with learning) in the minds of *some* teachers, parents, policy-makers, so it will be worthwhile to clarify here what we mean by it. For there is every hope that it means something important to pupils – they even use the term, unsolicited: "I think I'd learn a bit more if it was a bit more active" (Ben, 11 years). Recently we asked some pupils who were in their last year of primary school what they wanted their learning in secondary school to be like; they often used the word 'active'. Similarly, if we turn to research studies of teachers' and pupils' perceptions of effective classroom learning, we find that they prioritise approaches such as: group/pair work; drama/role-play; storytelling and drawing (Cooper and Macintyre, 1993). Does this give us an indication of what they mean by 'active'?

And why is activity related to learning? One part of the answer is that it contrasts with passivity. As one of Britain's top thinkers said in 1926:

> Wherever it is possible, let the student be active rather than passive. This is one of the secrets of making education a happiness rather than a torment. (Russell, 1926: 203).

Eighty years later there is good reason to take this point seriously. Surveys conducted by MORI of over 2,500 secondary school pupils in England between 2002 and 2004 (Campaign for Learning, 2006) showed that potentially 'passive' activities such as copying and listening had remained high or even increased. When asked "Which three of the following do you do most often in class?" the replies were as shown in Table 6.1.

Table 6.1 Pupils' most frequent classroom activities

Activities	2000 (%)	2002 (%)	2004 (%)
Copy from the board or a book	56	63	61
Have a class discussion	37	31	32
Listen to a teacher talking for a long time	37	37	39
Take notes while my teacher talks	26	20	20
Work in small groups to solve a problem	25	22	23
Spend time thinking quietly on my own	22	24	24
Talk about my work with a teacher	22	16	18
Work on a computer	12	10	20
Learn things that relate to the real world	11	12	14

We will consider what has led to this picture later in the chapter, but let's first clarify the notion.

Active Learning: What Do We Mean?

Definitions always have limitations, but they can be valuable for clarifying our focus. As part of a project examining active learning in eight countries, Simons suggested:

> All learning is active in a certain sense, but some kinds of learning are more active than others. Here active learning is defined in one sense to mean that the learner uses opportunities to decide about aspects of the learning process. A second definition of active learning connects it to mental activity in another sense: it refers to the extent to which the learner is challenged to use his or her mental abilities while learning. Thus active learning on the one hand has to do with decisions about learning and on the other hand making active use of thinking. (Simons, 1997: 19)

An important implication of this definition is that it takes our attention towards the learner's experience and what they do with that experience, including their own decisions about it. So we cannot take active learning to mean some simple version of the phrase 'learning by doing', which is fortunate because there are so many examples of humans continuing to 'do' without any learning taking place!

Indeed, classroom life can sometimes feel like 'Do, Do, Do' – and when you've finished that, do some more! We need to examine how the doing leads to learning.

In Simons' view of active learning the focus is on decision-making and thinking, but we also want to include the idea that the learner is actively manipulating materials of some sort, ranging from the kind of things that science teachers talk about as 'hands on', to the actual construction of objects as with design technology, to the creation of a musical performance, and so on. Nevertheless, the initial point still stands: we need to highlight the meaning-making which must be associated with the activity in order for us to be convinced that learning is taking place.

So we need the *experience* and the *means to transform it* in order to create knowledge. And here the role of reflection is crucial – indeed instead of the phrase 'active learning', it might be better to speak of 'action-reflection learning'.

> It is not sufficient simply to have an experience in order to learn. Without reflecting upon this experience it may quickly be forgotten or its learning potential lost. (Gibbs, 1988: 9)

So for active learning to be a part of effective learning learners need to be reflecting on their experiences, and for effective learning in classrooms one part of this must be the *ways in which pupils make sense* of what they are experiencing.

For the purposes of this chapter, we will take the term 'active' to mean engaging one's energies in various ways:

Behaviourally	*actively using and creating materials*
Cognitively	*actively thinking, constructing new meaning*
Socially	*actively engaging with others as collaborators and resources (a theme to be developed further in the following chapter)*

Activity and Effective Learning: What's the Link?

Below you will find some quotations from four different people writing about learning. They all make some sort of connection with activity. Read through to create your own view of what these people think is the link between activity and learning. As you read, try to clarify your own view of what that relation is.

Learning is a constructive process that occurs best when the learner is actively engaged in creating her or his own knowledge and understanding by connecting what is being learned with prior knowledge and experience. (Lambert and McCombs, 1998: 10)

Learning is an active process. A great deal of academic learning, though not everyday learning, is active, strategic, self-conscious, self-motivated and purposeful. Effective learners operate best when they have insight into their own strengths and weaknesses and access to their own repertoire of strategies for learning. In recent years this type of knowledge and control over thinking has been termed metacognition. (Brown and Campione, 1998: 178)

Students learn best when they actively construct their own meaning. During the last decade, cognitive psychology has embraced a constructivist philosophy. In this view students learn best when they are actively engaged. They are not blank slates, but rather are thinking beings bringing to each new situation prior knowledge, beliefs and dispositions. For real learning to occur, students must activate their prior knowledge structures or schemas and examine new information in the light of their past beliefs. Where new information is discrepant, students need to reconcile these discrepancies. Towards this end, students are encouraged to formulate questions, hypotheses, and predictions and then collect evidence by designing and carrying out experiments, doing investigation, and conducting library research. Throughout this process, students will either confirm or re-formulate their beliefs. (Baron, 1998: 217)

Two themes of the constructivist approach are particularly relevant to school reform: *active learning* and *learning in context*. Active learning refers to the idea that people learn by engaging in a process of sense-making. This process requires the learner's orchestration of a collection of cognitive processes ... Hands-on activity is not necessarily the same thing as active learning. Instructional methods aimed at active learning seek to engage the learner's cognitive processes, such as helping the learner select relevant information, organize that information into a coherent representation, and integrate that representation with existing knowledge. Instructional methods that emphasize learning by doing can sometimes stimulate active learning, but may sometimes stimulate rote learning. The goal is not to provoke behavioral activity per se, but rather to provoke productive kinds of cognitive activity. (Mayer, 1998: 368)

Having read these four contributions, which elements are most meaningful to you? How would you complete your own version of the statement 'Learning is an active process because …'?

The focus in these comments is clearly about the activity (mainly 'mental') in which a learner engages while constructing new meaning. The axioms of this view of learning are:

- Knowledge is actively constructed by the learner, in relation to previous knowledge, and not passively received from the environment (teacher, books, and so on).
- Coming to know is a process of adaptation based on and constantly modified by a learner's experience of the world. It does not discover an independent, pre-existing world outside the mind of the knower.

As others put it: Learning is '… the process whereby knowledge is created through the transformation of experience' (Kolb, 1984: 38). This already indicates the core role of a learner in *creating*: whatever the experience is, the process of making sense and developing new understandings is centrally the role of the learner. This view of learning helps us to make sense of findings which can be puzzling when viewed from an orthodox teaching perspective. For example, when a learner *creates* explanations it is usually positively related to achievement, while *receiving* explanations from other people is inconsistently and weakly related to learning (Webb and Palincsar, 1996). And when learners receive a response that has no elaboration, it is usually negatively related to achievement (Webb, 1989).

This view of learning and the importance of activity for learning also sheds light on the way that in classrooms some learners learn to become passive. Detailed studies of the way that different students' questions are responded to by teachers suggest that for those students who the teachers see as low ability, they come to ask fewer questions, and thus learn to be passive. 'Eventually they learn that it is better to avoid responding than to risk indicating that they do not understand' (Good et al., 1987: 194). So roles of activity or passivity are learned in the classroom – therefore they can be developed in the classroom.

Variations in Active Learning

1 A variety of tasks

If we keep in mind the aspects of active learning which have been clarified above, we can probably find applications in many of the different tasks which operate to promote learning in classrooms (reading, writing, and so on). Some brief descriptions are offered below.

Active reading

To be an effective learner when it comes to reading, a learner might need to go much further than the dominant (but passive) idea that reading is 'getting this text in my head'. A richer experience with the text, generating richer meaning as a result, is likely if someone engages actively with a text through strategies such as:

Scanning (before reading identify what's the theme, how is the text structured?)
Questioning (what do I already know, what do I want to know more about?)
Reading (small steps at a time, stopping at regular intervals)
Reviewing (what is being said, what do I think of it?)
Recollecting (what are the main messages, what are the key ideas?) (after Robinson, 1970, and others)

Such strategies are mentioned as possibilities, but they typically appear in 'study skills guides' as necessary. Yet some readers will be active and effective without necessarily using these: the main strategy of an active reader is the monitoring of how their reading is going, so that they never meet the situation of reaching the end of a page and saying to themselves "nothing has gone in"!

Again these points may be expressed by learners themselves. When asked what would need to happen for their reading to improve, children's responses emphasised activities including reading, talking and developing interest:

"Children should be given a chance to read every day."
"Teachers should ask them about their interests and help children find books on the subject."
"Teachers should recommend good books and talk about them."
"Children should have opportunities to talk about favourite books with each other and the teacher." (Roettger, 1978)

Active writing

Composing an effective text requires many thoughtful processes, as well as the practical and organisational skills of getting writing done. Less skilled writers approach writing as a 'knowledge-telling process', in which knowledge is little influenced by its translation into text (Bereiter and Scardamalia, 1987). It's a sort of dumping onto paper. By contrast more skilled writers approach the act of writing as something which in itself enhances their knowledge and understanding. It is for this reason that they do not pronounce it any easier a task (Scardamalia and Bereiter, 1991), since they are formulating more complex problems, advancing their knowledge still further and so on, in a feedforward loop that generates better but not easier writing.

Active writing can be supported through writers becoming more planful and reflective, using sentence openers of the sort adopted by skilled writers in planning (e.g., 'This isn't very convincing because …' 'My own feelings about this are …', and 'No one will have thought of …', (Scardamalia et al., 1984). Active writers also see the process of drafting as crucial: having developed an idea of what they want to say in text, they compose a draft, try it out with a reader and see whether it communicates what they themselves were intending.

Active listening

Teacher sometimes say that their pupils are poor at listening, but rather too often this refers to listening to teacher, and suggests that pupils are not complying, i.e. they are not being passive. But perhaps the problem is the other way round: ineffective listening is characterised by passiveness – of the mental sort.

Even in the most inactive of situations in a physical sense – the lecture – a learner can be listening in a way which involves actively raising questions, having new (internal) conversations, noting down new ideas and questions, and so on. So they can be an active and effective learner for that context, especially if they also review the experience once they have left. And of course if they even get a two minute break in a lecture, their learning is enhanced (Ruhl et al., 1987).

Active experimentation

The very phrase 'experiment' seems to suggest activity, whether it's a thought experiment, a scientific experiment, or a social experiment. So the active seeking of knowledge through trying something out is a very powerful process – indeed some evidence suggests that it is a defining characteristic of adolescence. Whether the experiment is highly planned in advance, like the sort of science which is taught in school, or whether it is a very open-ended experiment, this is a key way of gaining knowledge. The effective experimenter designs their intervention well, knows how to seek evidence and how to interpret it.

Active inquiry

Sometimes what we want to learn about is not amenable to experimentation in its fullest sense, and we wish to understand possibilities in a field by other forms of inquiry. Perhaps simulations, games and role-plays are relevant here, where an imaginative form of experimentation is possible within a safe context. The active inquirer frames their questions well, and can critically evaluate the forms of information which might be gathered. For effective inquiry in any of its many different levels the development of these skills is important.

2 A range of scale

There are many ways that active learning can be employed in classroom life, and they vary in scale: from the brief, individual activity which may take no more than a few minutes of a particular lesson, to a cross-disciplinary project which engages multiple students and staff for a term. In each the same process and principles apply.

It is perhaps the case that the 'larger' the task, and the longer the time, and the more people involved, the more complex are the processes to be handled in active learning. But by the same token they are more authentic each time. Nevertheless it is common for teachers to start with the small scale.

3 A range of subjects

A few brief examples are offered in Table 6.2 to make the point that active learning is not the province of a particular area or school subject. As you read across these few words, the active sense of creating new knowledge may come across.

Table 6.2 Brief examples of active learning in a range of subjects

Subject	Do	Review	Learn	Apply
Maths	Tackle a problem	Review strategies	Compare effectiveness	Prepare for next challenge
English	Create a draft	Try out with a reader	Consider feedback	Redraft and publish
Technology	Construct a product	Test its function	Examine evaluations	Redesign
Drama	Rehearse	Critique	Adapt	Perform
History	Collect sources	Identify points of view	Synthesise	Make sense of another situation

Active Learning: A Core Process

The conceptual similarity between the examples offered above is at the level of a similar process which informs them all, a process which can be described as a cycle. This cycle models the process of learning from experience with four phases: Do, Review, Learn, Apply (Dennison and Kirk, 1990). To this we also add the important stage before doing – planning – to give the model in Figure 6.1.

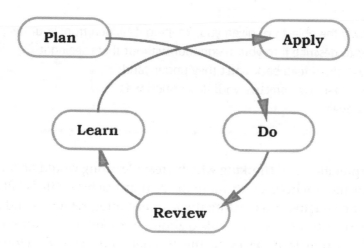

Figure 6.1 A model of the activities involved in a learning process

This model can be used with learners of all ages. The first three words of this process – Plan, Do, Review – have guided the very successful 'High/Scope' approaches to early years classrooms (Vogel, 2001), and these approaches have been shown to have beneficial effects lasting into young adulthood. The model 'Do Review Learn Apply' features in the UK's 'Schemes of Work' for teachers of Design Technology in secondary schools. For adult learning also this core process is recommended: The National College for School Leadership's New Visions programme emphasises the recurrent nature of this cycle:

> Action enquiries follow a cycle of learning, such as: plan, act, observe, reflect or do, review, learn, apply. Once one cycle is completed another begins. (Cotton et al., 2003: 17)

The model may label parts of a process, but this is not meant to imply that they are completely exclusive or in some sense separate boxes. Rather they highlight the different aspects of experience which compose a process of active learning, so that we can get the sense of what is needed to learn from experience. And it's important to remember the point about multiple cycles: active learning is not some magic formula for one-trial learning – rather it accumulates and empowers as everyone becomes more practised in it.

Facilitating the process

It's at least theoretically possible that a teacher could 'instruct' an active learning cycle. For example, in this brief activity as a paired communications exercise:

Plan: Study the object I've given you, keeping it hidden from your neighbour.

Do: Try to describe it to your neighbour without them seeing it.

Review: Have them feed back what they understand.

Learn: Consider how effective your description was.

Apply: Try again.

But the interpretation and thinking which create learning would be hidden here (at least from the teacher), so it's more likely that teachers will facilitate active learning by encouraging and eliciting the learners' interpretations and meaning-making. When such processes are talked about 'out loud' they gain more meaning. So in an action learning cycle the teacher's role may develop by them prompting the learners at each stage.

Here we list some generic prompts, which would be selected and fine-tuned for a particular activity:

In the 'Do' phase:
Key Question: 'What is happening?'
- What do you see/notice?
- How do you feel and think about that?
- What else is happening?
- What's changing?
- What's going best?

In the 'Review' phase:
Key Question: 'What do you think?'
- What struck you about that?
- What did you see operating there?

- What's the most important thing that happened? Why?
- How was that significant?
- What difficulties did you meet? How did you resolve them?
- What strategies seemed effective? Why?
- What else could we have done? How might it have been different?

In the 'Learn' phase:

Key Question: 'So what?'

- How did you make sense of that?
- What does that mean to you?
- What might help us explain that?
- What might we draw from that?
- Does it connect with anything else for you?
- What does that suggest to you about … in general?

In the 'Apply' phase:

Key question: 'Now what?'

- Where does this leave you? Where does this take you?
- Do you know other situations like this one?
- What have you learned about those situations?
- Will you do something different next time?
- Have you developed a plan?

Can you imagine an activity which you currently use in your classroom which could be developed into more effective active learning by the use of such prompts?

Active learning: roles for teachers and for pupils

In order to get more activated learners we need the learners to be involved in activating the classroom. This is a change in the balance of roles, but does not leave the teacher without a role! The balance of roles in a classroom may be positioned at any point on this continuum:

Learner Activation ⟷ *Teacher Activation*

When teachers make a shift in their role on this dimension, various advantages follow. Active learning reduces teachers' work – or rather shifts it into a different script. Active learning engages the energies, understandings and motivations of learners themselves, so it can be associated with reduced stress for teachers.

In making the shift towards more active learning in the classroom, teachers may start by trying out particular activities or methodologies. Occasionally they may get stuck there, but this would still be a teacher-activating approach. As we build in more opportunities for learner activation (they come fairly naturally in the later stages of a learning cycle anyway) the relations between learners and methods, and consequently the teachers, begin to shift. As Kane puts it:

> the success of an active learning methodology depends not on methodology alone but, ultimately, on the constantly-evolving, dialectical relationship between methodology and learners, mediated by the educator. Practical implications are that educators need not be over-obsessed about questions of methodology. (2004: 275)

But when the classroom roles do shift towards more learner activation, a further advantage is reflected in the evidence that student performance improves.

Evidence of Effects

An early study into the effect of active learning not only gave important results but also used an ingenious method which illustrates a recurring theme in this book. Benware and Deci (1984) wanted to compare students who learned with an active orientation with students who learned with a passive orientation. The active orientation was created by having a student learn material with the expectation of teaching it to another student; the passive orientation was created by having a student learn the same material with the expectation of being tested on it. The results indicate that students who learned with an active orientation were more intrinsically motivated, had higher conceptual learning scores, and perceived themselves to be more actively engaged with the environment than subjects who learned in order to be examined.

Other early studies used the device of randomly assigning students to treatment or control groups, and teachers to classes in the treatment groups. To study the effects of active participation on student learning, 500 11-year olds from eight elementary schools were given a 30-minute lesson on probability, and the treatment group used demonstrations-practice-feedback, and structured activities. A test immediately following showed better results for the active learning groups (Pratton and Hales, 1986).

The view of learning which informs the importance of active learning ('constructivism', as described above) has informed large surveys. Abbott and Fouts describe a (2003) study of 669 classrooms (a representative sample of classrooms drawn from humanities, maths, science, and English classrooms). A strong relationship between constructivist teaching practices and student achievement on state tests was found.

Another large study of nearly 5000 students between the ages of 9 and 14 (Newmann et al., 2001) showed that students who received assignments requiring more active and challenging intellectual work also achieved greater than average gains on the state test of basic skills in reading and mathematics, and demonstrated higher performance in reading, mathematics and writing on other state tests. Contrary to some expectations, high quality assignments were found in some very disadvantaged Chicago classrooms and all students in these classes benefited from exposure to such instruction.

These studies have emphasised the point made by Mayer at the beginning of this chapter – that it is not behavioural activity per se which leads to effective learning, but the intellectual activity which is stimulated at the same time. A constructivist lesson is less dependent on specific teaching strategies and more dependent on the types of intellectual demands placed on the student.

The evidence that teachers who adopt beliefs and practices along the lines of active learning get better results in various performance measures than those who do not now covers a range of countries and age groups; for example 6 year-olds in the USA (Peterson et al., 1989), teachers of 9 year-olds in Germany (Staub and Stern, 2002), 10 year-olds in Japan (Inagaki et al., 1998), 11–13 year-olds in the Netherlands (Biemans and Simons, 1995), and secondary school students in a whole state of the USA (Abbott and Fouts, 2003). Even at university level, studies show that active learning brings better results in short-term measures. Students in a history class who participated in role-play did better than their traditionally taught peers on a short written test a week later (McCarthy and Anderson, 2000).

Perhaps more importantly, active learning can have a constructive effect on learners' ways of going about their learning. Even in a context where previous experience has not been characterised by active learning, students report it making a valuable contribution to the development of independent learning skills and the ability to apply knowledge (Sivan et al., 2000). On an established measure of learners' approaches to study, an increase in deep approach was found, i.e. a focus on underlying meaning. Studies which have examined the association between approach to learning and exam performance give a further value to these findings, showing that strong effects come from learners activating their own planning and their own reflection. In the UK, the GCSE scores of pupils who plan and reflect least are just 30 per cent of the scores of the pupils who plan and reflect most (Atkinson, 1999).

On a wider point about the purposes of school, children in an experimental active learning programme in some rural schools of Guatemala showed significantly more democratic behaviours than their counterparts in traditional schools (de Baessa et al., 2002). Within the active learning programme, greater democratic behaviour and small group participation were also related to higher reading achievement at the classroom level. Both were seen as especially important achievements for emerging democracies and 'developing countries'.

Voices Against Change

In Chapter 4 we identified some of the ways that the 'official voice' of government and its agencies can have a negative effect on classroom practice and effective learning. Here, and in each following chapter, we identify some more local voices which may operate against this theme. These are voices which circulate in our own thoughts and conversations as teachers. It is worth identifying these and examining them, so that any unwitting power they may have can be challenged and they can be examined in the light of other voices, including the voice of evidence.

On the theme of active learning, many teachers' 'Yes, Buts' are fairly predictable (Geist and Baum, 2005). Here we mention a few which we have regularly encountered.

"I have to cover a prescribed curriculum."

Sorry? Who's covering the curriculum? Isn't it the students' task to do that? And the more active they can be in that task, the better the results (see the example in Chapter 5).

"It takes too much time."

Yes, when we feel under a time pressure, the temptation is 'to just tell them' (see John Sullivan's comments in Chapter 4). But the whole point is that telling in itself achieves nothing, and that even if you do tell them, the learners have do to something active to make their own sense of what you have told them. The time taken for learners to be active sense-makers leads to them achieving depth over breadth and gaining significant expertise on the topics.

"It'll all fall apart: the lack of structure will lead to behaviour getting worse."

Issues that centre around 'control' and our fears of 'loss of control' are often heard when talking about change in classrooms. But they unwittingly appeal to a fictional view that the teacher is in control of everything in the classroom! The teacher-centred classroom creates its own patterns: 'pupils' behaviour is highly visible, as is a teacher's treatment of pupils. This visibility stimulates high desist rates as well as creating 'demands of equity' that force a teacher to rely on commands' (Bossert, 1977: 561). In other words lot's of 'Don't!' from teacher, and lots of 'That's not fair' from pupils. When there is more active learning the locus of control changes; partly towards the learners, but mainly towards the activity itself. The teacher is less the centre of public attention, and their role is less about monitoring behaviour. Detailed studies of the patterns of disruptive episodes in classrooms show that there is more difficulty during whole-class teaching (Lawrence et al., 1989).

"It seems like a lot of work."

To begin with it may seem like that, especially as teachers learn to plan differently and in a way which their previous routines do not support. But as the shift continues the time spent on planning for active learning reduces, and time can be spent on the more important matters of learning. The same happens in the classroom itself. The number of demands which learners make of the teacher can reduce dramatically. The *type* of demand also changes. In one study, before the classroom changed almost two-thirds of the pupils' requests were to do with evaluation or transitions: afterwards these were only one-quarter. Instructional requests increased from one-twentieth to one-fifth of the total, as learners became involved with 'higher level' demands on the teacher's time rather than with more mundane requests (Bennett and Dunne, 1992).

"The students don't want it."

Yes, on some occasions if you offer students a choice of something different, they will stay with what they know in classroom life, especially if they get the idea that the teacher is going to abandon them. But when it comes to being more active in their learning, students regularly voice their wish in such a direction, and are critical of the teacher voice which says that students don't want it!

> Some students said that "teachers think that students cannot use active learning methods; but students can; they could learn if teachers were able to apply these methods". Students considered that the main weakness is the teachers' lack of capacity to use these methods, not the students' lack of capacity. (Niemi, 2002: 774)

We do not want to suggest a 'blame game' between students and teachers, and this disappears if students can focus on their learning and study, rather than just on the classroom:

> In assessing if students felt that the active learning techniques improved their ability to study more efficiently, students were overwhelming positive. As they described their experiences, the new techniques created a cycle which made them feel more secure and led to more efficient studying and more effective studying. (Qualters, 2001: 55)

Nevertheless it's good to know that very similar doubts can arise for students. Their old orientations sometimes die hard: for example, after eight months of experiencing techniques to promote active thinking, two students came to their science teacher. One said: "We see what all this is about. You are trying to get us to think and learn for ourselves." "Yes, yes" replied the teacher, heartened by this long-delayed breakthrough, "That's it exactly." "Well", said the student, "We don't want to do that" (White and Gunstone, 1989).

"The parents wouldn't like it – they want me to 'teach' their children."

Is that a fact? Or a surmise? Yes, many parents may seem to want a traditional classroom style, especially if they have been made anxious and they think their child's fortunes are at risk. It is no surprise given the fact that they are likely to know no other way. But ask them about their own experience of classrooms and they will tell you it was best when it was active, so you may be able to get them 'on side'.

"My colleagues wouldn't like it – it'll be too noisy."

Since the fifteenth century silence has been seen as a characteristic of a good classroom – it's a reflection of the classrooms which were located in monasteries. Some teachers may make the same judgement today. But more often it's a judgement which seems to creep out of the woodwork when we're feeling anxious about doing something differently. Active learning is not necessarily any noisier at all – there can be long periods of quiet when the engagement is high. But this voice does remind us of the importance of colleagues when teachers experiment with classroom practice.

Teachers Making the Change

For many years it has been recognised that change in classrooms does not come about through merely advocating it. John Dewey spotted that the practice of telling does not change by merely telling!

> Why is it that, in spite of the fact that teaching by pouring in, learning by passive absorption, are universally condemned, that they are still so entrenched in practice? That education is not an affair of 'telling' and being told, but an active constructive process, is a principle almost as generally violated in practice as conceded in theory. Is not this deplorable situation due to the fact that the doctrine is itself merely told? (Dewey, 1916: 38)

Eighty years later, a researcher looking at students preparing to be teachers concluded that even direct experience may not be enough. Following an active approach in seminars,

> ... most students' views of teaching and learning changed little between the beginning of the seminar and one year later. Most believe learning is a reflex of teaching; most say they would lecture to students despite the fact that their own experiences of lectures are overwhelmingly negative ... (National Center for Research on Teacher Learning, 1993: 5)

Perhaps these understandings illustrate why some researchers (for example Niemi, 2002) talk of 'a cultural change needed in teacher education and schools'. While this may be the case, a possible hazard is that teachers may think the culture is not under their influence or will wait for it to change before making experiments. More positively, the notion of cultural change may alert us to the fact that teachers who develop more active approaches often do so collaboratively. Small groups of teachers who start by observing classrooms (either live or through video examples) and discuss what they see regularly find that their focus moves from teaching to learning, and then become supportive of reflecting on and experimenting with their own classroom practices. In the process they may try out new approaches with each other, or be facilitated to do so, and this direct experience can be important:

> Teachers need to experience this kind of teaching themselves in order to successfully adopt the pedagogy. It was not until the experimental course for practicing teachers provided the opportunity for teachers to engage in conversation about both another's pedagogy and their own pedagogy that the participants were able to understand how to teach for active engagement in learning. (National Center for Research on Teacher Learning, 1993: 5)

But we should not altogether ignore the matter of individual teachers who make real change, sometimes because of transforming events. We met one secondary school teacher in Birmingham who said "I changed my teaching methods overnight." We said "From our understanding of how classrooms change that's pretty unusual – can you convince us?" "Yes", she said, "I did a 'pupil pursuit' [following a pupil or pupils on their experience of school for a day] and when I saw what their day was like I vowed never to contribute to anything like that again." Her classrooms became much more active as a result.

That teacher felt that she could do what she saw best, and reflected a sense of autonomy. This will be important in helping change. In countries where there has been development of a distinctive pedagogic style, 'teachers have been given considerable autonomy at the classroom level' (Ramsay, 1993: 29). So in countries like the UK, where a teacher-centred prescriptive style of classroom has become more common, teachers who develop more active learning have found ways to win back autonomy at the local level of their classroom. It is curious that government-centred prescriptive policies echo the more dominant nineteenth century versions of classrooms (Campbell et al., 2003), while at the end of the twentieth century international studies of quality in teaching have stressed the importance of active learning for students (OECD, 1993).

What do you see when action learning is happening?

One other element in making the change is having a vision of what the classroom will come to look like and using that vision (rather than the dominant ones of teacher instruction) to evaluate progress. The framework of headings from a constructivist stance offered in Chapter 3 (page 35) may help to maintain the focus.

As we come to the end of this chapter and its focus on active learning, we now turn to another dimension of promoting effective learning in classrooms which has often been just below the surface of this chapter. We move now from active learning to interactive learning.

Collaborative Learning

Classrooms are crowded and busy places, so potentially very social. Yet when it comes to talking about learning in classrooms, much of the talk is about individual learning – it's as though the social aspect did not exist. This paradox has the effect of marginalising the social nature of classroom life, or at worse turning it into a problem because it appears to divert from teachers' goals – for individuals. Yet when we ask teachers about their best hopes for life in their classrooms, they talk about the social aspects, the relationships, the climate. So there's a submerged view amongst teachers that classroom learning would be improved if the social nature of learning was embraced and the social arrangements of the classroom were to enhance the learning. In such a context effective learners would necessarily be supported, since learners inevitably have to engage with others.

In this chapter we aim to clarify what collaboration is, examine how it can enhance learning, and explore how it is best managed in the classroom.

Did the best experiences of classrooms, which you were invited to think about in Chapter 1, make any reference to the social interactions, social relationships and social climate? If so, how was it that they contributed to such a positive classroom?

Collaboration – What Do We Mean?

The essence of the term 'collaboration' is to labour together, not with a sense of hard toil we hope, but with a sense of creating something greater between us than would have been achieved separately. Although the literature is not completely consistent on this, some writers maintain a distinction between cooperation and collaboration (Galton and Williamson,1992; Tiessen and Ward, 1997). The distinction suggests that people are cooperating when they adjust their actions so that each person achieves their individual goals, whereas people are collaborating when their actions are adjusted in order to achieve a shared goal. By way of a classroom example, imagine four pupils round a table: they would be cooperating with each other if they needed to share resources for each to complete their individual task ("pass the ruler please"), whereas they would be collaborating if they worked together to create a joint product ("let's build it like this").

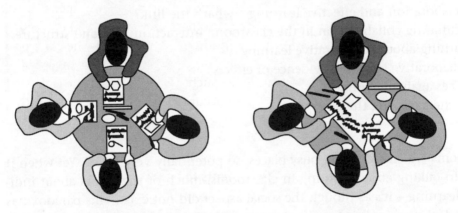

Figure 7.1 Images of cooperation and collaboration

Do the different images in Figure 7.1 highlight anything about your current experience in classrooms? Often we might see pupils grouped around a table: sometimes that's as far as it goes – a furniture arrangement. On other occasions they may be cooperating, in order to complete their individual tasks. It's those other occasions when they are collaborating on a shared task which form the focus for this chapter.

We can highlight two main characteristics of collaboration:

- During collaboration something new is created that could not have been created otherwise.
- Collaboration takes place when all the participants can contribute to a new shared product.

Thus communication is a key element for cooperation and collaboration to happen.

Collaboration and Effective Learning – What's the Link?

The link between collaboration and effective learning is dependent on the sort of talk which takes place between the participants. Talk is a core human process, and human learning is centrally about meaning, which we create and exchange through our use of language. In contrast the learning of other animals does not have this feature, nor indeed do the reductionist behavioural models of learning which were transposed from the study of animals (Shuell, 1986). A focus on meaning and talk draws us to consider the way that communication occurs. Before we move on to look at communication in collaboration, it is worth noting that this focus helps us understand individual examples also: if a learner explains things to her/himself, greater understanding develops, even in apparently solitary processes such as reading a text (Chi et al., 1994).

As a first step in collaboration, many studies show that when learners explain their meaning-making to each other their learning is richer and deeper. The act of having to make sense to a peer challenges someone to clarify and communicate in such a way that their own understanding is enhanced. In the classroom context, therefore, a building block is the use of pairs who are involved in exchanging or co-creating explanations. In such conversations, the *process* of explaining is all important, not the status or accuracy of the explanations. When learners are practised in such discussion, those who are deemed 'low ability' are successful in helping those of 'high ability' to extend their learning (King et al., 1998 – contrary to some government guidance in the UK). In such settings it takes a reasonably short time for improvements to occur, for example in critical thinking (Gokhale, 1995). And one person may promote effective learning for another by prompting a conversation that creates understanding together, including self-explanation (Chi, 1996).

The key process which links collaboration and learning is well expressed by Annie, a 10 year-old talking with Caroline Lodge:

> "You learn more [when working with others] because if you explain to people what to do you say things that you wouldn't say to yourself, really. So you learn things that you wouldn't know if you were just doing it by yourself."

Annie has captured here the key idea which was previously and perhaps more famously expounded by Vygotsky (1978): it is that new knowledge and ideas develop in a context of dialogue, and they appear first 'out there' in the extra-mental plane. We find ourselves saying things that we have not said before, and may later consider them in the light of our existing ideas – on the intra-mental plane. Many teachers recognise this process for themselves, as it arises in their teaching, especially when they find themselves offering yet another explanation to students, and saying it in a way that has not occurred to them before.

From our starting point of explanations, we can identify some of the other principles at play in collaboration. Any learner has the capacity to communicate to another their explanation of something (although whether they will do so may be dependent on the quality of the classroom climate in which they find themselves – a 'right answer' climate will hamper the exchange of explanations). When someone does offer an explanation, they act as if they believe that they have something comparable to bring to the shared context. When that happens, they find the situation pleasurable (Crook, 1999). And with these ingredients, the social and the intellectual start to work together: relationships and meanings start to grow.

At the same time, another dimension may come into play, which in this example could be how learners will cope with their different explanations. Handling differences in a way which remains collaborative (not conflictual or combative) is crucial for the dialogue to produce further meaning. If learners are involved in a task that really demands collaboration, they will have to bridge multiple perspectives on the problem, and create a common ground through language. Under these conditions their discourse becomes more thoughtful and conceptual than does that of individuals working alone (Schwartz, 1995).

So the twin building blocks of collaborative tasks and processes are:

- Bringing together something comparable on a theme or a topic.
- Reconciling multiple perspectives through the medium of dialogue.

Do your experiences of collaboration and learning reflect these twin building blocks?

Facilitating Collaboration in the Classroom: Interaction, Task and Structure

Facilitating collaborative learning in a classroom involves a number of aspects, both planned and responsive. Those which may be planned include three related aspects:

- Promoting collaborative interaction
- Designing collaborative tasks
- Building collaborative structures.

Promoting collaborative interaction: thinking together and acting helpfully

There's no reason to assume that putting learners into groups and giving them a joint task will necessarily lead them to collaborating. Their previous classroom history and much of their surrounding culture may not have prepared them well, and (as various research studies show – see for example Mercer, 2002) the interaction may be disconnected or even competitive. Part of the solution is to be found in the design of the task, but another necessary part is the sort of interaction we encourage.

The pattern of interactions between learners in a classroom is not fixed: it can be altered by teachers and their design of the classroom environment. From time to time we might need to encourage skills of discussing, skills of helping, skills of thinking together, and so on. A range of classroom studies has shown that this can be facilitated by offering learners the sort of prompts which help them generate the appropriate interaction, and thus learn the skill in the process.

Some prompts focus on the thought-provoking aspect of interaction. For example:

"Why is ... important?"
"What would happen if ...?"

Students who used such prompts with each other and answered each others' questions showed greater understanding (King and Rosenshine, 1993).

Other prompts invite peers to examine one's reasoning:

"What do you think of my idea?"

or to voice what has been understood of others' explanations:

"So you reckon that ...?"

Still within this realm of ideas, the issue of how to handle differences arises, and other prompts are valuable. Here tentative language is used:

"It might be that ..."
"It seems that ... "

Similarities as well as differences are acknowledged, and disagreements are framed in terms of ideas not persons. In all this, multiple stances are assumed:

"From this point of view ... "

Other prompts focus on the social aspects of interaction. On those occasions when a teacher allocates particular roles within a cooperative group, for example a 'doer', a 'reviewer', and an 'encourager' (Cohen, 1994; Chalmers and Nason, 2003), prompts for how best to enact each role may be placed on cards in order to publicly clarify the roles and help students understand how their individual role might be enacted.

With collaboration, learners become effective help-seekers and effective help-givers. Help-seekers can explain their confusion and ask specific questions for help, so this may perhaps be supported by practising prompts such as:

"I'm confused about … "
"I don't see why … "
"It would help me if you could explain … "

Help-givers can check whether their explanations have been understood and whether confusions have been clarified.

Other prompts are helpful to support learners in addressing the emotional aspects of their interaction, when the clear communication of emotional states is especially helpful, for example:

"I feel … when you … because … "

This encourages learners to make 'I statements' rather than accusatory statements.

Prompts to promote collaborative interaction can be brought into the classroom in a range of ways: spoken by the teacher, written on cards, and also generated by learners themselves as the process develops. But collaboration is not only influenced by the participants' understanding of interaction; it is also called out by certain types of task.

Designing collaborative tasks: connected, high-level, relational

The design of the task given to a group of learners has significant impact on whether they collaborate with each other. There are some obvious pointers to follow. The task must not be 'decomposable', in other words capable of being broken down into parts which group members can complete alone – especially into a single part which one group member can tackle while others engage in what has come to be known as 'social loafing', and waiting for someone else to do the work. So it would be counter-productive to give a group of learners a set of maths exercises, for example, since one person could complete them for the rest.

And we need to consider a second characteristic:

A group task has two characteristics. First, it requires the resources (information, skills, materials) that no single person possesses; success on the task requires the contribution of many … Second, there must be interdependence, and the interdependence between students must be reciprocal. An interdependence in which better students always aid weaker students is a one-way dependence. Interdependence is reciprocal if each student is dependent on the contributions of all others. (Cohen, 1992: 5).

The question now becomes how to promote interdependence through the task. If a task is to do this, it cannot be a 'right answer' task: instead, tasks for collaboration are often described as 'higher order thinking', in that they require a thoughtful approach and the negotiation of meaning. So if our group of learners was asked: "Look at these maths exercises, see whether there are different ways of completing them, and decide whether one way is better than the rest", the task would necessarily involve them in variety, strategy and decision-making. Their interaction would need to bring their perspectives together and reconcile them together. As their experience of doing this grows, so would their quality of collaboration, but the point here is that the characteristics of the task play their part. Over time, research indicates that:

> groups which deal with ill-structured, non-routine, discovery-oriented tasks become more productive as interactions increase because mutual interchange is a necessary condition for solving the problem. (Cohen, 1992: 5).

Such tasks can be devised in any knowledge area and for any age of learner.

In the examples above, the task has included an intellectual dimension and a social dimension. The social dimension asks learners to communicate and agree. How they do this, and whether they complete it, are dependent on whether the learners have adopted the goals which the teacher has given them. It is possible to make collaborative classroom activity more effective and more interdependent by the task (also noted in Chapter 6) of pupils teaching each other. The goal of helping a peer learn involves both social and intellectual dimensions, and is somehow more self-motivating than teacher-provided tasks. Collaborative tasks which are based on teaching each other are likely to incorporate higher level thinking and mutual interchange. This principle has been built into the classroom structures addressed in the next section.

Building collaborative structures

The typical classroom shows little sign of structuring its participants to promote collaboration between them. As we saw in Chapter 3, pupils' drawings of classrooms often depict them as isolated learners. These often show a layout of rows or a seating plan based on gender or attainment, indicating that these learners are not arranged to view each other as resources for learning. But some simple structures can have considerable effect, as evidenced in the literature for decades.

The basic building block is pairwork. Through brief and focused conversations, peers get the opportunity to voice their thoughts and start a dialogue about them. Such classroom practices are called many things in schools: 'chatterboxes', 'talk partners', 'study buddies' and so on. The development of the interaction which is central to such practices is helped by the prompts mentioned above. And its further development is aided by review (to be addressed below). But the key point here is that pairwork forms the bridge between private thoughts and public discussion (see Figure 7.2).

Private   Peers   Public

Figure 7.2 Peers as the bridge between private and public

That simple but important principle forms the basis for a structure called 'Think Pair Share' (Lyman, 1981). In its original version this starts with a teacher's question:

- **Think** about the question individually.
- **Pair** up with a partner. Explain your answer and listen to your partner's response.
- **Share** your answer (or your partner's) if called upon.

This structure promotes the sort of talk and interaction which are needed for collaboration, but it does not as yet create a collaborative product, and remains mainly controlled by teacher. A further development was called 'Formulate-Share-Listen-Create' (Johnson et al., 1991). The important addition here is to ask learners to create something collaborative after the earlier steps have been followed through:

- **Formulate** your answer to the question individually.
- **Share** your answer with your partner.
- **Listen** carefully to your partner's answer. Note similarities and differences in your answers.
- **Create** a new answer that incorporates the best of the ideas. Be prepared to present your answer if called upon.

With this building block of pairwork, a variety of structures is available. In a structuring practice which developed from research into helping with literacy, an important shift occurred from teacher setting the questions to pupils generating them. From an analysis of the strategies used by competent readers, approaches were devised for developing these (Palincsar and Brown, 1984). The approaches were then built in to the collaborative structure known as 'reciprocal teaching' in which pairs or small groups of learners, sometimes with and sometimes without their teacher, hold a discussion about a text.

- **Question**: about the content of the text, re-reading where needed.
- **Summarise**: to identify the gist of what has been read and discussed.
- **Clarify**: concepts or phrases which are unfamiliar or a source of confusion.
- **Predict**: the next part of the text.

In early versions of this practice a teacher might demonstrate an example of this style of conversation, and then in pupil pairs one pupil would act as the teacher for the discussion. We find that this role specialisation is not always needed. Also in some versions the questioning phase can come before the reading, and the order of phases in the pairwork can be adjusted too. For example:

- **Question**: What does this reading seem to be about? What do you already understand about this topic? What more do you want to know?
- **Clarify**: What did you each take these authors to mean?
  What did you do with hard-to-understand parts?
- **Summarise**: What are the main messages?
  What are the key ideas?
- **Predict**: What might happen if these ideas were taken forward? What could you do in using them?

So a collaborative structure of pairs or small groups is built up, using a high-level meaning-making task, and over time the pairings and group roles are changed. In the process the core role of the classroom is handled through a more distributed structure: everyone is teaching everyone else. The principle of the 'reciprocal teaching' structure can be applied to a wide range of ages and classroom tasks (Kelly et al., 1994).

From the building block of pairwork, we now move to consider methods of structuring whole-class collaboration. These are quite rare in the typical classroom. Whole-class plenaries or whole-class discussions are very often of the form where learners' comments are directed to and managed by the teacher, and in these circumstances it is rare for members of the class to engage in dialogue with each other. Some simple tactics can help to develop from this state of affairs more of the process needed for collaboration. For example in a 'round robin' structure where individuals or small groups are making contributions to a whole-class discussion, having a practice whereby any contribution has to be prefaced by some thoughts about the previous contribution can lead to more connection and flow. But even this process is not yet one which necessarily develops collaboration, in that a product created together does not necessarily emerge. Again, simple tactics might provide a step in the right direction: if a class has spent time creating in pairs, their product may then be brought to small groups of four or six in which further dialogue and learning take place. Then the small groups come together to create a whole-class product. This structure has sometimes been called 'snowball', because the product increases in size as the process rolls on. In such structures the small groups are usually focussed on the same task, so the variety is low: this can lead to the later stages of the conversation sometimes feeling like repetition rather than dialogue, so that a minority of pupil voices (sometimes the usual minority) are dominant. Also, the later stages can easily slip into 'reporting back' views, rather than contributing these to a collaborative whole-class product.

An alternative whole-class structuring practice which overcomes these difficulties has its history in the context of improving race relations in the 1970s in the USA, following the desegregation of schools (Aronson et al., 1978; Aronson and Bridgeman, 1979). Rather than trying to solve the difficulties which arose between black and white students by bemoaning their lack of skills or by creating 'add-on' strategies from programmes, the inventor took the view that core classroom activities needed to be addressed:

> it would be valuable if the basic process could be changed so that youngsters could learn to like and trust each other – not as an extracurricular activity but in the course of learning their reading, writing, and arithmetic. (Aronson, n.d.: 8)

An approach was devised which could apply to any classroom activity that can be divided into component parts – a story, a reading, a production, a new area of knowledge. The metaphor of a jigsaw is used to describe the whole class making up a picture from its parts. The classroom practice is to divide an area of enquiry into different sections, each one of which is allocated to a sub-group of the class (Aronson and Patnoe, 1997). In Phase I, these sub-groups become temporary experts in their section, and then in Phase II the groups are recomposed with one expert from each section in the (now) 'jigsaw' group (see Figure 7.3). At this point the big picture is created – through students who have now created a grasp of that picture through their own efforts and understandings.

Jigsaw methodology is used in all phases of education and importantly builds a

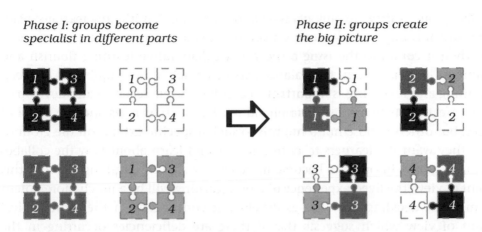

Phase I: groups become specialist in different parts

Phase II: groups create the big picture

Figure 7.3 The structure of groups in a jigsaw classroom

climate of interdependence in the classroom, as each person's activity is necessary for their colleagues to be able to learn. In Chapter 5 we described how Andrew Nockton handled the performance and coverage pressures through his use of this jigsaw methodology in his secondary school history class.

To operate a jigsaw classroom with the numbers typically found in many classrooms, say 30 students, various alternatives are possible for the formation of groups. Obviously a topic which can be divided into six areas allows six specialist groups of five students in each, which on recomposing can become five jigsaw groups of six students in each. In this example, a single student from each specialist group travels to each jigsaw group. Other possibilities emerge if we think of students travelling from their specialist groups *in pairs* to the jigsaw groups. For example, a topic which is divisible into five areas allows five specialist groups of six students each, which on recomposing can become three jigsaw groups of ten students each. Although a group size of ten may be more than usually planned for, there are five specialist voices in this group, which helps manageability, and each is represented by two students. This latter aspect is commented on very favourably by participants, who feel that the responsibility for getting the specialist contribution they bring from their temporary expert group 'correct' is shared in a constructive way, and the act of moving with a partner is experienced as a collaborative support.

Learning about Collaborative Learning

Collaborative learning in classrooms will not happen unless teachers play their part in planning for it, and the above sections have indicated three areas in which planning is of value. But we should not fall into the current trap of believing that plans are everything – they are only plans – nor of believing that it's only teachers' planning which is important – learners' planning is crucial too (see the next chapter). So when it comes to the issue of how will collaborative learning flourish and maintain in a classroom, the balance between teacher and pupils and between planning and reviewing is important to consider. Some teachers and developers go to great pains to arrange beforehand matters such as roles and the detail of tasks, but others choose not to do this to such a specific extent, on the grounds that they want the learners to notice, review and learn about how the collaboration is going, in order to become more empowered in handling it. From this point of view, the lived experience of group learning will be a much more potent element in deciding how things develop. It contrasts with the more typical point of view which suggests that if there are deficiencies occurring in the process of collaboration then it is a teacher's responsibility to teach learners some skills. So if collaborative learning is to develop in a classroom there must be occasions for review, along the lines of the active learning model described in Chapter 6, and part of the meta-learning to be described in Chapter 9.

When we come to review the experiences of collaborative learning in our classroom, some of the following prompts may help:

> *Our group work is best when …*
> *It helps us to collaborate when …*
> *Things that hinder our collaboration include …*
> *What did you notice about the way you all talked together? What were the best bits for your learning?*
> *Was there an equal chance to talk?*
> *How did you handle disagreements?*
> *Did the task help? How?*
> *When we do this next, what can we improve?*

In examples we have witnessed, the richness of pupils' comments can come as a surprise to teachers. For example, Yvonne, a teacher in a North London school, was asking a class of 6 year-olds about their experience of Talk Partners, which had been new to the class just a few weeks previously. One comment highlights the way that a discourse about their learning builds in a collaborative fashion through the process of dialogue:

> "I didn't have a clue how to do it at first, but then my partner helped me. After he had told me about his work I knew what sort of things to say about mine."

And the effects of the discussions were noted, not only for 'remembering' but also the implied change to a more empowered learner's role:

> "Talk partners are good because then I can remember the work better. When we have to do it again I will remember it better and I won't have to ask the teacher."
> (Kurz, 2003)

Examples of reviewing reciprocal teaching have asked 10 year-olds how recipro-cal teaching has helped their learning. Answers included:

> "It has helped me to understand books better."
> "I feel like I can be a teacher as well. It makes me think about the book and ask questions."
> "It gives me confidence to ask other children questions and gives me independence." Maharasingam, 2004)

That last point is echoed by other learners when they review 'jigsaw' method-ology:

> "Ms X usually helps us learn a lot, but with this project it was different. A lot of the time I didn't even notice she was there. This has helped me learn that I don't need someone telling me what to do to learn well." (13 year-old: Timbrell, 2004)

And from this same class, we hear comments which confirm that the criteria for partnerships which adolescents often hold dear ('friends') can be superseded when the classroom promotes interdependence and a focus on learning:

> "The small group I was working in didn't really have any of my friends in it. By working with these other people, I have learned that it doesn't matter if you like someone or not, you can still learn from them. It has made me feel more open about listening to other people and other teachers I don't usually like." (13 year-old: Timbrell, 2004)

These comments have been included to support the idea of classroom review, but they reflect some of the findings from more formal research. In a secondary maths classroom which operated with cooperative learning groups, the matter of group composition was studied to find 'Most students indicated that they liked working in groups and appreciated getting help from other students, espe-cially for learning difficult concepts. Some students disliked having groups pre-assigned and permanent, and they suggested alternating group membership' (Whicker et al., 1997: 42). Another study (Hogan, 1999) showed that embedding 'Thinking Aloud Together' into a 12-week science unit with four classes of 14 year-olds led to a greater understanding of collaborative reasoning and a greater ability to articulate the collaborative reasoning processes.

The comments above also start to identify some of the benefits emerging from classroom collaboration and which have been researched in many contexts.

Collaborative Learning: Evidence of Effects

Research on the effects of collaborative learning is very extensive, and much of it has taken place in classroom contexts. Reviews of this research are regularly undertaken, and one much-quoted example listed 44, then 59, and now 67 benefits of collaborative learning (Panitz, 1999; 2000). In summary, the list covers:

- *Improved learning and achievement:* higher level thinking skills, student satisfaction with the learning experience, positive attitude toward the subject, less divergence between learners' achievements, learning orientation rather than a performance orientation, critical thinking and dialogue.
- *Improved skills:* oral communication skills, empathy skills, social interaction skills, self-management skills, leadership skills of female students.
- *Improved engagement and responsibility:* active involved exploratory learning, student responsibility for learning, student retention.
- *Improved relationships:* responsibility for each other, the classroom as a community, positive race relations, diversity understanding, student-staff interaction and familiarity.
- *Classroom resembles real life social and employment situations:* students wean themselves away from considering teachers the sole sources of knowledge and understanding.

The point here is not to make collaborative learning seem like a panacea or a miracle, but the evidence does affirm the benefit of taking the social aspect seriously, both as a core element of learning and a core aspect of classrooms. Indeed if a further step is taken to operate a classroom as a learning community, the positive benefits are perhaps greater (Watkins, 2004, 2005).

Voices Against Change

"They'll never cover the content!"

Here comes 'coverage anxiety' again, but slightly differently from the last chapter where it was 'I have to cover the curriculum'. We hope that with examples like Andrew's in Chapter 5 we can now see that there's an increased chance of 'covering' the curriculum and – more importantly – in depth.

"But they're going to get individual marks?"

True enough: this is one outcome of treating our education system as a device for grading and selecting individuals, whereas achievement at work is more of a collaborative affair. There are two points here: the first is that pupils get better individual grades when they have learned through a collaborative process; the second is that for the purposes of running your classroom, you might experiment with group grades. Others have found – contrary to expectation – that students value this: 'When given safeguards both to ensure fairness and to develop a grading system, students typically choose to have group work account for the largest share of their grade (usually over 50%)' (Michaelsen, 1999).

"Some of them couldn't collaborate in a month of Sundays."

Don't allow this voice to put you off experimenting because you may miss out on some big surprises. Like Gemma, a science teacher in a large London comprehensive, who after just a few sessions of collaborative work with one class with a poor reputation for behaviour saw that behaviour improved markedly as the engagement was raised

"I don't know enough about groups, especially when they're not effective."

But the knowledge doesn't have to be with you. You can learn about groups with the pupils, as they learn too. That's the reason for the focus in this chapter on the process of review. If we wait to become experts in groupwork (should such a thing exist) we may miss out on a lot of learning.

"The caretaker wouldn't like me re-arranging the furniture."

Well, perhaps its good to be clear who is in charge of pedagogy! But this can be a real issue, especially in secondary schools where many teachers operate in the same room. Again collaboration is a resource: a class of pupils can rearrange furniture in a very few minutes – and put it back again at the end.

Teachers Making the Change

Each of the things which can work against the development of more collaborative learning in classrooms gives us an indication of how we may progress and make changes in our own classrooms:

Yes, there are features in the context of schools and society which do not support, but studies of context also show how an understanding of contextual features can enable educators to improve the processes and outcomes of cooperative learning and other powerful educational innovations (Jacob, 1999). We need not expect the context to give us a lead. And after some time and some collaborative work with other teacher-colleagues, we may find ourselves more in the situation where collaborative classrooms are helped by a supportive collaborative climate in the school (Shachar and Sharan, 1995). But we are probably best advised not to wait for that to happen before we start!

Yes, many teachers say they have little experience of running a collaborative classroom, or indeed of having been in one. In the UK it is doubtful whether teachers' collective knowledge about collaborative classroom practices is as great as a decade ago (Rudduck and Cowie, 1988; Cowie and Rudduck, 1990). So we need to build that experience step by step, starting small and with a manageable level of risk.

Yes, pupils at first will show that they too are inexperienced in helping each other learn:

> Students adopting the role of help-giver showed behavior very similar to that of the teacher: doing most of the work, providing mostly low-level help, and infrequently monitoring other students' level of understanding. The relatively passive behavior of students needing help corresponded to expectations communicated by the teacher about the learner as a fairly passive recipient of the teacher's transmitted knowledge. (Webb et al., 2004: 1)

Yes, some studies highlight the lost opportunities for collaboration in classrooms (Murphy and Hennessy, 2001), but these alert us once again to the negative effects of too much focus on the product rather than supporting the process towards an even better product.

Yes, there are questions about how much the typical classroom designs its activities to be collaborative (McManus and Gettinger, 1996), but the purpose in this chapter is to suggest the key issues for this design.

Yes, some teachers do approach collaborative work as though it was a 'how to' procedure and 'lethal mutations' are abundant, for example in Reciprocal Teaching (Seymour and Osana, 2003) when there is a lack of understanding about the learning principles upon which the method is based. So if we keep our practice of collaboration as understood within the context of a focus on effective learning, we may get the best results.

As with other developments in classroom practice, teachers making the change find their role changing, and it is important to anticipate this. In one project, 15 teachers monitored the *demands of their pupils* prior to and after they had set up cooperative groupwork. The *average number of demands fell dramatically*, from over 38 per lesson to less than five. It would appear that the group could, in fact, handle most of the demands that individual pupils would usually make of teachers, and they in turn said 'Much more time was available to teach rather than to deal with many matters which can be peer assisted', 'it is a management method that really frees the teacher … ' (Bennett and Dunne, 1992: 54).

As the teacher's role shifts 'from sage on the stage to guide on the side' (King, 1993: 30), the style of planning also changes, and this may mean more planning time for the new style in its initial period. But there is a trade-off between any extra planning time needed and other benefits, such as less time correcting lessons, increased student motivation and fewer attendance and discipline problems.

These same benefits emerge from the practices to be considered in the next chapter, where one element consists of the idea that it's important for pupils to be doing some of the planning.

Learner-driven Learning

No-one else can do your learning for you. They may be able to support your learning by the way they manage an environment, or the way they talk with you, but they can't do it for you. And perhaps the other side of the same coin is put by B. B. King (American musician, b.1925): "The beautiful thing about learning is nobody can take it away from you." So the learner is always at the heart of the process, no matter how it goes.

Yet the way learning is talked about in classrooms, in contrast with other environments, seems to suggest that it's someone else who does it for all the pupils. Even pupils themselves get carried along by this sort of talk. We heard one story of a teacher who said to his class "I'd like you all to point a finger into the air, and when I ask you a question, turn your finger to point at the answer. The question is 'who is responsible for your learning?'." The whole class pointed their finger at him. After a few moments of noticing this a few fingers started to waver, but the point was made. These pupils were giving evidence of their view of learning in classrooms: the teacher is responsible, and they do not see themselves as having much of a role, let alone driving it. We tried a similar brief enquiry with a Year 7 class: in the context of a discussion about various aspects of learning, we asked the simple question "Who's responsible for your learning?". The answers came back, in this order "teachers", "parents", "governors", "the government!"

This chapter examines the ideas and evidence for changing classrooms away from the scenario where learners get a diet of 'uninvited teaching' (Holt, 1991: 128). In the process it contributes to creating a classroom situation in which pupils are more crew than passengers. And it describes a shift to a learner-centred view, moving away from the sort of teacher-centred view which would take 'independent learning' to mean "they go away and quietly get on with what I tell them!"

What are your starting thoughts on the theme of learners taking more responsibility for their learning? Have your best experiences of classrooms contained an element of this? This chapter aims to support you with ideas and evidence for developing classroom practice further.

What Do We Mean by Learner-driven Learning?

There are many different terms we think of when addressing the theme of this chapter, and none of them is perfect. We are not going to aim for perfection in language, since this area can get itself so lost in terminology that no development occurs. Here are some of the candidates in the field, together with a quick comment on each as to their suitability for describing the theme of this chapter. We want to consider classrooms which promote:

- *autonomous learners*: this term is often (mis)read to mean individualised learners, or learners in a lone context
- *learner responsibility*: sometimes used with a 'finger-wagging' connotation as though we should morally criticise learners for not taking responsibility
- *learner agency*: a good term, but not used widely enough to be accessible
- *independent learners*: here we usually mean 'more independent from teacher', which is a fine-enough goal, but we want to promote interdependence among learners (see the previous chapter)
- *self-regulated learners*: a term widely used in psychological literature, but regulation alone can seem like a constraining process rather than a driving process
- *self-directed learners*: reasonable but some folks say that this feels like a linear, always pushing forward description, whereas learners might sometimes need to retrace or recycle.

We have chosen to use the term 'learner-driven' to indicate the focus. It's a dimension of effective learning which focuses on learners choosing and deciding and planning and reviewing – that is, steering their own process. But again it's imperfect, as it could conjure up an image of the 'driven' learner!

With all of the terms above it is possible for people to reject them by creating simple polarisations as though it were 'all or nothing'. For us it's more 'a matter of degree', rather than there being some absolute that we are aiming for. In the complex social situation of a classroom one thing is always affecting another, and that applies to the various goals, purposes and directions of pupils and teachers. But we want to consider the ways that a classroom might somewhat shift the degree to which purposes and processes are determined away from the dominant teacher-determined patterns. As Seymour Sarason notes:

> In several elementary school classrooms I arranged for observers to be there from the first day of school to the end of the first month. I was after what I described as the forging of the classroom's 'constitution' – Who wrote the constitution of the classroom? The answer – to which there was no exception – was that the teachers wrote the constitution. They articulated the rules and regulations (frequently post hoc) but provided no rationale. There was absolutely no discussion of the rationale ... It never occurred to these teachers, who by conventional standards were very good, that students should be provided with a rationale, which deserved extended discussion, and that students should have an opportunity to voice their opinions. (1990: 82)

Why should we be wanting to shift the degree to which learners drive the learning? There are gains for teachers, for pupils and for the achievement of classroom goals. To begin with, for the teacher what is peculiar and perhaps paradoxical about the situation which Sarason describes is that it makes things more difficult for teachers and their role, mainly because all the responsibility landing on teachers' shoulders is potentially stressing. At worst it leads to defensive teaching (Chapter 4) or to adversarialism between teachers and pupils. And we have also seen that if teachers are given the major responsibility for classroom outcomes (as in some versions of 'accountability') they unwittingly recreate the conditions in a classroom which emphasise teacher control and which lead to poorer performance.

When teachers are told to get pupils to perform to high standards (as opposed to being told to help them learn) they become more controlling, and give more directive critical feedback. Although this can lead to some short-term performance gains, when the teachers are not present and the pupils are given choice, those students with 'helping' teachers perform very much better (Deci et al., 1982). The early laboratory studies of this phenomenon have been confirmed by studies in the natural context (Flink et al., 1990). A group of 15 primary school teachers was randomly allocated into two groups. All of them taught their 10 year-old classes the same two tasks, but in two different conditions: teachers in the first group were told their job was to help the pupils learn, while teachers in the second group were told that their job was to ensure children performed well. All teaching sessions were videoed and analysed by independent judges. Student performance on the tasks taught and on a generalisation task was assessed by independent judges. Results showed that the students did less well on the subsequent test when they were exposed to pressured teachers using controlling strategies as a result of the performance instruction.

So for students, a learning context which rarely asks them to make choices, guide the process, and evaluate their progress is hardly a good formative experience for adult life-long learning. But this does not mean that we are proposing the classroom suddenly becomes entirely 'free choice'. Indeed, children themselves do not seek this. Even young children express views along the lines of *"I want to make my own choices ... sometimes"*, showing that they recognise limits and appropriacy in context (Daniels and Perry, 2003; Daniels et al., 2001). Older students also express the wish to exercise more choice, even when their school career has not promoted autonomy in learning. One study of first year university students in Hong Kong concluded:

> First, students have far more positive attitudes towards learner autonomy than we would expect ... Second, ... there were clear indications of a general readiness for autonomous learning. The research results are useful and fairly unpredictable given the fact that these learners have little or no previous autonomous learning experience nor have they received any kind of preparation or learner training in this direction at the secondary level. One could imagine that learner autonomy is a totally new idea and experience to most of them as they have come from traditional, authoritative backgrounds. (Chan, 2001: 294).

These forms of evidence challenge occasional teacher comments such as "these kids can't make sensible choices" or "these kids don't want to make choices." We need to work against both comments, so that classrooms become places in which learners learn how to make effective choices – where appropriate – and at the same time develop the important competence of getting themselves to do some things that they have *not* chosen.

In this chapter the link with learning is the important rationale. Perhaps such choice has always been a feature of classroom life, but not in its best developed way:

> Students in all classrooms have always had the power to make the most basic choice about their learning: they may choose to engage in learning or to disengage. We cannot remove that choice. (Starnes and Paris, 2000: 392)

What's the Link with Effective Learning?

Effective learners are not people who are acting as if following a recipe. Even though some authors and packages may suggest it, there is no single strategy a learner employs which makes for effective learning – except for the meta-strategy of reflection and review. So what is the effective learner doing? They are directing some of their awareness to notice how they are going about their learning, and with this are occasionally stopping to ask themselves whether it's going well. Self-direction and self-regulation are at the heart of being an effective learner. *"When I'm stuck, I go back and check instead of guessing"*, says Vikesh (11 years). In saying this he offers us a hallmark statement of the self-regulated learner. Vikesh is able to monitor how things are going, identify experiences such as 'being stuck', and at that point he sees choices for himself. 'Going back' is the crucial quality – the ability to *re-trace* experience (which can only be done if you were in touch with it in the first place) and refer to other sources ('checking') as he does so. He knows this is more effective than the strategy he used previously (and could perhaps still use now in certain circumstances) – guessing. So effective learning includes this extra crucial ingredient which actively involves the student in the meta-cognitive processes of planning, monitoring and reflecting (Watkins et al., 2002). And this has to go beyond the idea that it is a simple skill for teachers to teach their pupils: teachers can teach as many skills and strategies as they like, but unless learners are actively and personally involved in planning, monitoring and reviewing their learning, these will not be effective.

From this perspective it will be no surprise that those who have analysed the research on classrooms which promote this dimension of effective learning address issues of control:

> Self-regulated learning (SRL), as the three words imply, emphasizes autonomy and control by the individual who monitors, directs, and regulates actions toward goals of information acquisition, expanding expertise, and self-improvement. (Paris and Paris, 2001: 89)

Self-regulation and self-direction have a core relationship with human motivation:

> Choice and the opportunity for self-direction appear to enhance intrinsic motivation, as they afford a greater sense of autonomy. (Ryan and Deci, 2000: 59)

Here we are using the sometimes risky term of 'motivation', risky because it often enters teacher talk as a deficit discourse – "she's not motivated" – but what is at risk is the type of motivation which operates in classrooms. We probably all know the cumulative effect of a lack of learner direction in the classroom:

teacher tactics then focus on extrinsic motivation:

> Completion of assignments according to teachers' standards then becomes the primary concern for students, rather than authentic integration of useful knowledge. The tragic effects on the learner of this transformation in education only further more of the same teacher tactics. (Ryan et al., 1985).

And the cumulative effect on learners is noticeable: students who lack a sense of educational autonomy will typically choose less challenging and less demanding tasks (Boggiano et al., 1988). Further than this, controlling environments contribute to low achievement, anxiety, and student dependence on others to evaluate their work (Boggiano and Katz, 1991). But it can be otherwise, and the possibilities are in the hands of the teachers, with significant implications for students' learning. When students are given limited choice and told to solve a problem in one way, they do less well in later problem-solving than those who have been taught the same strategy but have been encouraged to develop their own (Boggiano et al., 1993). Curiously (and sadly) students in the more controlling classroom viewed the teacher as more competent, despite their worse results: this element perhaps warns us that creating more learner-driven classrooms will also create a tension with traditional role perceptions.

So if we take the stance that students possess inner motivational resources that classroom conditions can support or frustrate (Reeve, 2006) then the challenge becomes a matter of how to achieve the best form of autonomy-supportive classroom with some learner-driven dimension. It is important to note that teachers can change and improve their practice on exactly this dimension, and as a result can achieve higher engagement on the part of their students (Reeve et al., 2004).

Facilitating Learner-driven Learning in the Classroom

When we come to think about how a classroom may be organised to promote learner-driven learning, there is not going to be a single or simple strategy, some sort of 'magic bullet'. There are classroom practices and approaches, but it's important to recognise that their use has significant implications for the balance of roles between teachers and pupils. To make this point, we'll start with some pointers about teachers.

To operate a classroom with learner direction (at least more than we find in the typical classroom) a teacher is likely to adopt a relational style that simultaneously communicates their belief in the importance of the learner, and serves to develop that belief in action. Studies which have analysed the differences between teachers who are high or low in autonomy support have made several interesting findings. Reeve et al. (1999) found that teachers who are high in autonomy support:

- listened to students more often
- allowed students to handle and manipulate the materials and ideas
- were more likely to ask about student wants, respond to student-generated questions, and volunteer perspective-taking statements meant to relay to the student the teacher's understanding of the student's emotional state
- were less likely to give solutions or use directives.

If pupils are to exercise more responsibility, the teacher may be able to play their role in that (apparently paradoxical) way where 'less is more'. As one reviewer puts it:

> students can be encouraged to assume some responsibility for school learning with less rather than more instructional mediation. This is not to suggest that teachers avoid planning. Rather it suggest that teachers avoid *over-engineering*, through gradually released control of certain processes and objectives. (Corno, 1992: 80 emphasis in original)

To operate a classroom with increased learner direction is to seek the prize of greater engagement. As Perrone (1994) found, students of all ages and levels are most engaged when they:

- help define the content
- have time to find a particular direction that interests them
- create original and public products
- sense that the results of their work are not predetermined or fully predictable.

This will have implications for how we view other matters such as 'the curriculum'. Heo's (2000) analysis of classrooms as environments to support learner-driven learning included two principles: the first is to provide complex and authentic learning tasks and contents. This principle overlaps with what we have met in the previous two chapters: in order for learners to be active, collaborative and engaged, there has to be a high-level approach to knowledge that requires active processing, a range of contributions and interpretation. This was emphasised in Heo's second principle: to provide varied and multiple representation of knowledge. In other words to support and examine different approaches, methods and (where appropriate) understandings. Here we see that a learner-driven classroom is not likely to be operated as a 'one right answer, one right method' classroom.

Now on to classroom practices, with a brief overview:

> *In classrooms which promote learner-driven learning, pupils might be:*
> - Making goals their own
> - Making choices – of activities, within activities, when an activity is completed
> - Involved in planning how they will proceed
> - Given encouragement to offer commentary on their learning – talk aloud
> - Supported in reviewing their experience – tell the story
> - Evaluating the end-product
> - Motivated by internal purposes.

To emphasise, there are some key connected processes which recur in these practices:

- Purpose
- Choice and plan
- Voice and review.

Purpose and Choice

Choice is important, but sometimes the choices which inhabit a classroom are pretty unimportant: which pens to use, which table leaves first, and so on. For choice not to be superficial, it has to focus on the key purpose of the classroom – learning – and develop that purpose at the same time. The development of autonomy is not merely a matter of making choices which someone else offers to you. Meaningful choices cannot be made without a sense of personal relevance and purpose. In one study of 862 children and young adolescents aged from 9 to 14 years-old, the finding of purpose was more important than the provision of choice (Assor at al., 2002). So a classroom environment must also contribute to the development of young people finding purpose and relevance in their activities – including on occasions when those activities are not of their own choosing (Stefanou et al., 2004). Then teacher's action is seen by learners as autonomy-supportive if it helps them to develop and realise their personal goals and interests (Assor et al., 2002).

Conversely a teacher's action is experienced as autonomy-suppressing if it is perceived as interfering with the realisation of a child's personal goals and interests. So the development of personal goals and purpose is not a pre-destined process; rather it comes from active engagement with experience and environment. The classroom environment may profitably include such things as 'asking students to justify or argue for their point, asking students to generate their own solution paths, or asking students to evaluate their own and others' solutions to ideas' (Stefanou et al., 2004: 101). In these ways, learning tasks are structured to promote engagement, and interest develops *as a result*, rather than it being seen as the precursor to engagement. So in any area of classroom learning – whether or not it has been 'chosen' by learners – we may hear:

- What's *your* question about this?
- What's *your* explanation?
- What's *your* method?
- What's *your* interpretation?
- What's *your* next step/question?

A similar example develops from the practice which has become common in many UK classrooms, which is to write the 'learning objective' on the whiteboard. It's not a learning objective, nor even a teaching objective: it's a performance objective, usually written in the bureaucratic language of the official voice (for example 'Pupils should be taught to choose form and content to suit a particular purpose', and 'Children should learn that when the Sun is behind them their shadow is in front'). This practice has led to learners losing engagement or acting strategically, because it focuses attention on a pre-defined product and not on the process of learning. Ways for reclaiming learner engagement with such statements emphasise choice and purpose, for example through asking learners:

Look at the 'learning objective' and discuss in pairs:

- What could it mean?
- Who uses that?
- What might I be able to do with it?
- How could we best learn that?

In examples where we have seen this in action, especially those which are handled in pupil pairs at first, the dialogue is intense, the link to authentic experiences is rich, the development of purpose is marked, and the suggestions for how best to learn are practicable and engaging – and often beyond the repertoire which even a 'good' teacher would offer. Such practices contribute to the promotion and development of *intentional learning* (which for some long time has been put forward as the goal of instruction: see for example Bereiter and Scardamalia, 1989).

So pupils might make classroom choices on:

- What they learn
- How they learn
- How well they learn
- Why they learn.

Each time a choice is made, engagement is likely to increase, and learners set themselves a level of challenge which works for them. It is possible to start with small-scale choices, fitting within present practices, and then to develop these on a larger scale:

Choices in what to learn:
- Which of this set of problems will you begin with?
- Where in this text will you start reading?
- Which story shall we have read to the class at the end of the day?
- What questions do we want to address in this topic?

Choices in how to learn:
- Which reading place will you choose in the classroom?
- Will you present your recently-written account to others?
- How much shall we operate alone, in small groups, as a class?
- What activities will help us learn this best?

Choices in how well to learn:
- What can we do to make sure we learn the best we can?
- What would be some good indicators of quality in our end-product?
- How shall we demonstrate our understanding later on?

Learners' questions should come first. Although teachers sometimes hesitate, and take the more typical route of getting learners to start off by reading about a topic, there is good evidence that eliciting learners' initial questions about a theme leads to richer deeper questions than those raised after reading about the theme (Scardamallia and Bereiter, 1992). At a later stage, students choosing how best to demonstrate their understanding and devising questions to check their understanding fosters both depth and challenge. It also gives students more control, makes evaluation feel less punitive, and provides an important learning experience in itself.

- *What experiences have you had of classrooms where pupils exercise some meaningful choice and develop purpose? What new possibilities are starting to emerge for you?*

Choice and Planning to Learn

The above small-scale examples introduce the idea that pupils have an explicit role in planning their learning, and this idea can be developed to a larger scale, to such matters as content, method and the whole programme for a class.

- *Content*: In some examples (Passe, 1996) students choose the topics for study and thus play a part in curriculum planning.
- *Methods*: In other examples (Donoahue, 2003) 10 year-olds review the different classroom activities in their science lessons (experiments, worksheets, research, presentations, etc) and rate them for their effectiveness in promoting their learning. The following term is then planned with this in mind.
- *Programme*: In the most fully developed examples, learners are able to plan and organise extended periods of learning, including that which is a preparation for mandated tests (see the example, page 116: Starnes and Paris, 2000).

So there is a range of possibilities for engaging pupils' planning. As you consider such examples, it is likely that your current assumptions about learners and their 'ability' to plan their learning will come to light, and if we assume they have little ability we are likely to do the planning for them. But evidence suggests that even those students who are deemed to have learning difficulties, for whom a common strategy is for teachers to do even more planning in even smaller chunks, can show increased learning through being asked to plan their writing (Troia et al., 1999). So some of the common assumptions about how best to respond to particular learners may need to be reviewed. And the style of planning curriculum may need revision. Even from a teacher-centred perspective there has long been evidence that some styles of planning can be counter-productive: 'Planning to instructional objectives can lead teachers to limit their range of response to pupil contributions' (Arends, 2004). So from the perspective of promoting effective learners, there is even more need to find a better way, in which the focus for teachers' planning becomes key processes in the learner, and gradually helping learners to take this task on for themselves.

- *What examples of pupils planning their learning do you know? What new possibilities are starting to emerge for you?*

Voice and Review

The above practices have started to elicit learners' voices as a key part of learner-driven learning. Many learners will not be practiced in expressing their voice on classroom processes, but it soon develops and can be further developed and facilitated by classroom practices which promote review. So we now shift from choice and planning in advance of an experience, to review during and after an experience. These are processes which help learners notice more, and talk more about it. When the focus of the review is the experience of learning itself, which is addressed in Chapter 9; when the focus of the review is the quality of learning products, this is a major contribution in reclaiming assessment, and this is examined in Chapter 10. Here we focus more on the 'what' of the learning.

To continue our metaphor of 'driving' learning, we drive this by developing purposes and making choices, then as the process is under way we review and adapt to the effects of our actions and the circumstances. To mix the metaphors for a moment, we might call this 'in-flight' reviewing. And after the journey is over, we can review our drive again, but this time the quality of the review will reflect how much 'in-flight' review had taken place.

Prompts for such review relate to the task and topic in hand, but could be of the following forms, and handled in paired conversations:

In-flight review
- How is your approach working for you?
- Can you explain how it's going to a partner?
- How do you both rate those explanations?

End of journey review
- Did the different methods have different results?
- Did you have different interpretations? Can you justify them?
- How does this tie in with what we have learned before?
- What is a new example of this idea?
- In thinking about how it all fits altogether, are there any confusions?
- What do you think would happen if …?
- Is there some knowledge you are lacking now?
- How will you seek that knowledge together?

Clearly such prompts would be differently tuned for different ages, topics and activities. But the richness of such reviews will show up in more thoughtful choice and planning next time round, and with learners taking a much more engaged and active role.

- *What prompts for helping learners review have you tried? What new ones might you experiment with?*

Evidence of Effects

Through a range of research studies and accounts, there is evidence that learner-directed learning in school classrooms has positive effects on:

- Learner motivation
- Engagement
- Performance
- Behaviour.

Learner motivation, and engagement

Student orientation towards learning is a crucial aspect of motivation and is influenced by their classroom experience. When it is positive, students have a desire to develop competence and improve intellectually. This orientation is reported by adolescents when they perceive their teachers as using learner-centred teaching practices (see the survey of 4,615 students by Meece et al., 2003). Middle schools students also report more positive forms of motivation and greater academic engagement when they perceived their teachers were using learner-centred practices (see another survey of 2,200 students by Meece, 2003). So when the classroom is learner-centred, students develop a different orientation to their learning.

And similarly for student choice, when classroom experiences are authentic, allow choice, and demand student skills students find the quality of their learning experiences is high (in the 12 to 18-year range: see Yair, 2000). For these 865 students, randomly selected in 33 schools, there was considerable range in their ratings of current experiences. This confirms that it is the quality of the classroom experience (not some general tendency by the student) which has an effect on their motivation, engagement and learning.

When teachers are more supportive of autonomy and less controlling, students demonstrate higher levels of intrinsic motivation and self-determination. Intrinsic motivation is the wish to complete something for its own sake rather than for a 'reward' and is in line with the evidence that extrinsic rewards can undermine intrinsic motivation (Deci et al., 2001).

A learner-centred environment yields significantly higher achievement scores and a somewhat higher internal motivational orientation, even with students who are 'at risk' of dropping out of secondary school (Alfassi, 2004).

Performance

Classrooms which promote learner-driven learning are also associated with higher performance in public assessments. Mike Hughes (1993) operated his geography classroom with small groups, open access to resources, study guides, and so on. His role was to give regular small group and/or individual tutorials. Mike's geography colleague in this comprehensive school, Alan Cosford, taught a parallel group of Year 9 pupils in a traditional manner, and as an experienced and successful teacher was not threatened by comparisons. GCSE results for the more learner-driven class were 30% higher.

Large-scale research surveys confirm the point. The more students are supported as autonomous learners, the higher their school performance, as demonstrated by the grades in french, maths, biology and geography for 263 15 year-old students (Fortier et al., 1995). The connection between students having a self-determined motivation in school and achieving higher grades was confirmed in a later study of 1,623 14–15 year-olds (Guay and Vallerand, 1997). This study also showed that students were likely to have that important self-determined motivation in school if they perceived themselves to have autonomy in school, more so than if they perceived themselves as able in school.

The presence of mandated tests can demonstrate the power of learner-centred practices. Susan Moon starts her school year asking the class how they think they will have to organise matters to achieve the best they can in the state tests. The students devise a plan of creating lessons to teach to younger students. At the end of the year, the pupils scored the highest test results for her region in the first part, and second highest in the second part (Starnes and Paris, 2000). What is important about this example is that it is about pupils planning how best to achieve given goals: it is not about choosing subjects or choosing assessment.

Students who are engaged in planning have higher performance. One study of GCSE results (Atkinson, 1999) showed that the scores of pupils who plan least are just 30 per cent of the scores of pupils who plan most. Again the variation between learners reflected influences of the context, not fixed capacities 'inside' individual learners.

Behaviour

The fear which teachers sometimes voice – that student behaviour will worsen in a context of choice and learner control – is not supported by evidence, for example from Kaplan et al. (2002). In their study of 388 15 year-olds in 60 classrooms, a pupil orientation towards learning was associated with lower reports of disruptive behaviour, whereas a pupil orientation towards performance was associated with higher reports of disruptive behaviour.

Large surveys of these issues have been carried out in the USA.

> In national samples of more than 4,203 upper elementary and middle school students in rural, urban, and suburban schools, data indicated that as students' perceptions of their teachers' classroom practices became more learner-centered, not only did academic performance increase (as assessed by both teacher classroom grades and standardized achievement tests), but non-academic outcomes such as motivation to learn, school attendance, and school disruptions also improved. (Weinberger and McCombs, 2001)

A link has also been demonstrated with students' intention to drop out of school. The less autonomy supportive teachers, parents and school management are, the less positive are students' perceptions of competence and autonomy. In turn, the less positive students' perceptions are, the lower their levels of self-determined school motivation are. Finally, low levels of self-determined motivation lead students to develop intentions to drop out of high school, which are later implemented leading to actual dropout behaviour (see the data from a study of 4,537 students: Vallerand et al., 1997).

In summary, the practices and evidence in this chapter illuminate the links in Figure 8.1.

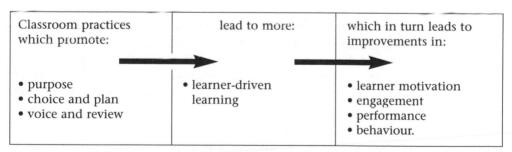

Classroom practices which promote:	lead to more:	which in turn leads to improvements in:
• purpose • choice and plan • voice and review	• learner-driven learning	• learner motivation • engagement • performance • behaviour.

Figure 8.1 Classroom practices and the effects of learner-driven learning

Voices Against Change

Teachers recognise the value of learner-centred classrooms and work hard to create them (Paris and McCombs, 2000). But they may have to work hard because there are many forces which operate against the creation of more learner-driven learning in classrooms. Recent evidence in the field of assessment for learning concludes that the majority of teachers found it difficult to promote learner autonomy (James, 2006). So it is useful to identify and anticipate some of the forces we may experience.

Occasionally the voices come through teachers. We have already mentioned comments such as "Kids can't have absolute freedom" (Where did that extreme suggestion come from?) and "They're not mature enough yet" (Will we wait forever or help them mature now?) and the occasional tendency to talk about pupils in terms of deficits – "They haven't got the skills" – rather than in terms of their experience – "We haven't helped them become competent in this yet." As we come to recognise these voices and their negative effects we can more often ensure that our actions are not driven by them.

But there are some wider forces which are also worth recognising:

- *The deep under-estimation of young people in our society.* Children and young people are regularly thought of in terms such as 'preparing for adulthood', in which they are seen as un-formed and un-ready beings. Their considerable powers are under-rated and under-used.
- *The fact that most of the practices of schooling are based on the idea that adults know best.* Adults write the curriculum, adults decide how the learning should happen, adults create the assessment, and on many occasions the official version of this adult voice does so with absolutely no reference to the learner.
- *It may feel difficult for teachers to promote autonomy in pupils if teachers experience little autonomy themselves.* Recent evidence from over 250 teachers across a wide range of school years confirms that they are hampered in their task by a sense of pressure:

  the more teachers perceive pressure from above (they have to comply with a curriculum, with colleagues, and with performance standards) and pressure from below (they perceive their students to be non-self-determined), the less they are self-determined toward teaching. In turn, the less they are self-determined toward teaching, the more they become controlling with students. (Pelletier et al., 2002: 186)

So the challenge in a context of performance pressures is how to respond in a way which still promotes learner autonomy. The impact on performance will be positive.

Teachers Making the Change

Many different things contribute to teachers making a shift towards more learner-centred learning, and sometimes they are not part of what the teacher was planning! Sally describes a Year 10 class who are not easy for her but at the same time she knows it could be advisable for them to be taking more responsibility and choice. She even has a mental image of what it could be like, but it doesn't happen. Then one morning, for a whole host of reasons, Sally arrives at the class less prepared than she would wish. She finds herself telling the group to choose between three options – and it happens! (with great engagement). Elizabeth is a maths teacher who happens to be delayed for one of her classes. On arrival in the classroom, she finds the whole class in a group discussion. Fortunately, she approaches quietly in order to listen in to the topic of discussion – it's about a television programme to do with mathematics which had been shown the previous evening! Elizabeth joins in the discussion in a very different role to the usual lessons, one of greater equity.

These two examples of how serendipity can play its part are significant for two reasons: first, each of the teachers took the opportunity which presented itself; second, each of them experienced some surprise as the classroom developed in a new fashion – and the world did not fall apart! It's often the 'fear of losing control' which holds teachers back from taking steps towards more learner-driven learning. Many teachers know that these fears are not well grounded, but they still have their influence, and as a result classrooms carry on in their predictable teacher-driven fashion. Writers in this area (Jeffers, 1997) encourage us to take the view that the fears may not disappear, but that they may be tamed (White, 1985) so that their negative influence is reduced. 'Feel the fear, and do it anyway' encourages us to experiment without waiting to feel comfortable.

The very strong emphasis on teacher planning which is to be found in some schools may make it feel paradoxical for the teacher to plan to give up their planning, but that is in some sense the task, in order to redistribute the planning. Making the change to a more learner-centred or learner-driven classroom is something which teachers tell us has an ongoing element of discomfort, and we should not be surprised to hear this as it is changing the script and culture of 5,000 years' worth of classroom history. But at the same time it offers a deep professional satisfaction, and a new set of learning relationships.

In many examples we have witnessed, some of which are included in this book, teachers who have been approaching the class with the intention of inquiry (especially inquiry into learning) tell us that the relationships between them and students improve.

In making a shift towards more learner-centred learning, we refute the notion that children are not learning unless teachers are teaching (Doan and Chase, 1996) and create a different script for the roles in the classroom, and a different future for classrooms:

Schools of the future must focus on developing skills for inquiry, reasoning, memory, creativity, interpersonal relations, metacognition, and perceptual control. (Areglado et al., 1997)

Further elements of this vision will be addressed in the next chapter.

CHAPTER 9

Learning about Learning

> *In this chapter*
> What do we mean by learning about learning?
> What's the link with effective learning?
> Facilitating learning about learning in the classroom
> Evidence of effects
> Voices against change
> Teachers making the change

It's a peculiar feature of life in classrooms and schools that there is not much talk about learning. Schools are sometimes called 'seats of learning' but can fail to live up to the title, instead appearing to operate as machines for teaching, with all the unintended effects this has. Is there much talk about learning in your school?

Yet with the information-rich and fast-moving world in which we live, learning about learning is an increasingly important capacity, which could be seen as every young person's entitlement in their education, with schools making this a very important contribution in the overall landscape of learning. But rather than preparing young people to be life-long learners, schools sometimes seem to be developing a life-long dependency on teaching. How would you rate your own schooling on this question? And how would you rate schools you know today?

When it comes to effective learning, as the appreciative enquiries we and you have carried out will show, many people (teachers, pupils and others) mention active, collaborative and learner-driven approaches in the classroom as the important ingredients. So the themes of the preceding three chapters are reasonably well experienced and discussed. People are less likely to mention the fourth theme which is to be addressed in this chapter: learning about learning.

Perhaps there is a simple reason for this state of affairs: it has less of a history, and thus is less developed in our classroom practice and our professional language. We teachers may not have experienced such learning ourselves. Reflecting on this, one senior teacher said "D'you know, I went through the whole of my school career and didn't notice a thing about my learning." Pupils are in a similar position: a recent study of the experience of 13 year-old pupils concluded 'Effective practices are encouraging activity in learning, learner responsibility and collaboration. Young people expressed a wish that their classroom experiences would include more of these elements. In all four schools, however, there does not seem to be any time for talk about learning' (Carnell, 2004: 6. See also Carnell, 2005). The results of this state of affairs were recently highlighted in a Scottish study which found that in the absence of a discourse of learning, young people saw themselves as 'pupil' rather than 'learner', and 'appeared to operate on an understanding that school work consisted of a fixed content of information or techniques for which they had to learn right answers and correct performance' (Duffield et al., 2000: 271).

This chapter will examine the various ways through which everyone could come to notice more about their learning, the classroom practices which support this and the evidence of its effects. It will adopt a particular stance on this developing field, amongst the many which are on offer.

What Do We Mean by Learning about Learning?

In our everyday language the term 'learning about learning' may have various connotations: for some it seems a distant, impersonal or bookish enterprise. That is far from what it means for us: in brief, we mean a learner learning more about their lived experiences of learning. That says a lot about a key issue we need to clarify at the outset here – which view of learning is being invoked. In schools, the word 'learning' may be heard in conversations and meetings, but much of it is a subtle cover for talk about teaching or results or schoolwork. So in these circumstances the phrase 'learning about learning' could regress to 'being taught to be taught', or the focus on results, or working smart. The real focus on learning disappears fast.

When we do start to focus on learning, the range of terms in current use can still show important differences. For example, take a look at the following:

- Thinking about Thinking (Collins and Mangieri, 1992)
- Learning to Think (Perkins et al., 1993)
- Learning to Study (Gibbs,1986)
- Learning How to Learn (Novak and Gowin,1984)

- Learning to Learn (Nisbet and Shucksmith,1984)
- Learning about Learning (Säljö, 1979; Watkins et al., 2000)

The first term in this list is also called 'meta-cognition' – awareness of thinking processes, and 'executive control' of such processes, a term only invented in the 1970s (Brown, 1975; Flavell, 1976). The last in the list is sometimes called 'meta-learning' (Biggs, 1985) – making sense of one's experience of learning. Just as learning involves a lot more than merely thinking, meta-learning covers a much wider range of issues than meta-cognition, including many issues about the goals, feelings, social relations and context of learning. And between these two the other terms in this list vary in important ways, as do the practices associated with them. Some adopt a highly instrumental approach to learning, carrying the message that if you learn these strategies (for example concept mapping, note-taking) you will be a more effective learner. Others seem to carry the message that there is a definable list of successful learning strategies which may be specified in advance for any learning, without reference to goals or purposes or contexts.

We do not adopt the stance which says that learning skills or strategies or techniques can be defined in advance and applied to any learning because of the evidence about effective learning.

What's the Link with Effective Learning?

It's not effective to teach learners particular strategies which are the supposed strategies of learning, for three main reasons. First, learners may come to 'possess' these strategies, but not employ them. Early investigators in this field noticed this after teaching a repertoire of strategies, and explained it in terms of children having no knowledge of their learning in which to locate these strategies. So new strategies may be taught but may remain as separated and disjointed practices. Second, some learners who may come to adopt the learning strategies employ them ineffectively. They may employ them in a routine manner which turns out to be maladaptive for the task currently at hand – "I always do a concept map this way." Here the process of selection and use of strategies are brought to our attention and the meta-cognitive strategies of monitoring and reviewing are vital – "Is this way of doing a concept map proving useful for this example? What else could I do?" The 'transfer' of a learned strategy from one context to another requires that the learner recognises the applicability of that strategy in the different-looking context (Halpern, 1998), again a meta-cognitive process. Reviews of research into the direct teaching of 'study skills' to students without attention to reflective, meta-cognitive development have concluded that it may well be pointless (Hattie et al., 1996). Indeed it may be worse than this: a third reason appeared in studies of teaching study skills to undergraduate students, where it emerged that when a group of students is taught that a particular strategy is good for learning, some of the students are saying to themselves "But I don't use that strategy – so I must be worse than I thought." Thus a well-meaning programme can have a negative and disempowering effect if it seems to suggest that there is only one way of approaching effective learning (Gibbs, 1981).

Extracting a positive principle from each of the three reasons above, we may see that to help learners become more effective requires:

• Helping them gain an understanding of their own learning (into which strategies might then take a place).
• Helping them develop skills of monitoring and reviewing their learning, paying attention to the goals and the understanding of their own processes.
• Maintaining the message that a diversity of practices can be effective for learning.

This sort of approach has been indicated in studies of meta-cognition, highlighting strategy which actively involves the student in meta-cognitive processes of planning, monitoring and reflecting (Biggs and Moore, 1993). Also, in stances on the 'expert learner':

> Reflection on the process of learning is believed to be an essential ingredient in the development of expert learners. By employing reflective thinking skills to evaluate the results of one's own learning efforts, awareness of effective learning strategies can be increased and ways to use these strategies in other learning situations can be understood. (Ertmer and Newby, 1996)

But the skills required are not solely individual in nature, as the term 'meta-cognition' sometimes seems to suggest: that's where the term 'meta-learning' encompasses the social nature of the situations in which we learn, and the social nature of our motivation to learn. Teachers readily recognise this, and display it when we ask "What can we see or hear someone doing who we believe to be an effective learner?" A selection of answers from teachers is given below, ordered under the headings which recur in this book.

Active in seeking understanding and connections
  Asks "Why?"
  Asks questions (comparative, analytic) about meaning
  Tests my (teacher) knowledge
  Says "How do you ... ?"
  Is prepared to suggest 'answers' without being sure they're correct

---

Can support a view 'opposite' to their own
Will ask and check about future applications
Is interested in a wide range of available ideas
Collaborative
Relates (discusses, talks about) their learning with peers/teachers
Asks for help
Good at connecting with you (teacher) in a quiet way
Exercises responsibility for own learning
Uses experiences of 'getting it wrong' to ask more questions
Proposes new strategies for advancing own learning
Approaches task in a strategic manner, regularly
Judges when they need to ask for help
Sets themselves challenges
Uses homework to revise class work
Displays meta-cognition
Says "I hadn't thought of that"
Says "I don't understand, and ... "
May change a point as he or she is going along

The point to note here is that despite the considerable limitation of only focusing on observable features, we can nevertheless see evidence when a learner displays thoughtfulness, not only in the fact that they make some of their thinking available by offering a commentary or 'thinking out loud', but also in the way they go about being active, collaborative and driving their own learning. But the limitation of focusing on observables does mean that we cannot have access to a key element – the learner's goals – unless, of course, they happen to talk about them.

So effective learners have gained understanding of the individual and social processes necessary to become effective learners. We have encapsulated these points previously and referred to them in Chapter 2, saying that learning is:

- an activity of construction
- handled with (or in the context of) others
- driven by learner's agency (these have also been reflected in Chapters 6 to 8), AND

  "Effective learning is all of these at their best, PLUS the monitoring and review of whether approaches and strategies are proving effective for the particular goals and context" (Watkins et al., 2002: 4).

In this section we have intended to show how learning about learning is a key element in effective learning, notwithstanding the fact that it is underdeveloped. The view of learning processes which is emerging here, and therefore the sort of knowledge an effective learner has about themselves, stands in contrast to a practice which has increased in some UK schools which its proponents suggest will help young people understand more about their learning. It is the approach which many schools and teachers have adopted of using 'learning styles'. Their adoption is understandable since there is quite a 'hard sell' of these ideas, and they seem to offer a quick and manageable strategy in hard-pressed times (see also our comments in Chapter 4). But we are fortunate that a massive review of the research on such 'learning styles' has recently been undertaken. On the technical issues, it concluded:

> some of the best known and widely used instruments have such serious weaknesses (e.g. low reliability, poor validity and negligible impact on pedagogy) that we recommend that their use in research and in practice should be discontinued. (Coffield et al., 2004a: 138)

The key point here is that the shift which occurs in all this talk of learning styles – from a focus on learning to a categorisation of learners – leaves out all the important processes which have been shown to characterise effective learning. Rather, we need to help learners understand more about their experience of learning, keeping a sense of diversity and without inviting them to label themselves. There is no gain in anyone coming to describe themselves as 'a visual learner', especially if they then select learning opportunities on the basis of this description: but there may be gain from a learner working out how to extend their strategies and approaches to the full range of 'styles', involving them in reflection, review and so on.

Facilitating Learning about Learning in the Classroom

When it comes to devising classroom-based interventions to help children become more effective learners, the contrasts made above have great significance. One of the earliest and most illuminating workers in this field, Ann Brown (an English-born woman who became one of those rare people to be honoured by both the American Educational Research Association and the American Psychological Association) conducted studies to identify the skills of effective learners, effective readers, and so on, and then set about helping children learn these skills in classrooms. Her summary findings are worth quoting at length:

> Trained to use a variety of strategies, such as classifying, organizing, summarizing, and so forth, children dramatically improved their learning performance. But there was a

catch: when left to their own devices, there was little evidence of continued use (maintenance) or flexible deployment (transfer) of these strategies.

Gradually it became apparent that children's failure to make use of their strategic repertoire was a problem of understanding: they had little insight into their own ability to learn intentionally: they lacked reflection. Children do not use a whole variety of learning strategies because they do not know much about the art of learning. Nor do children know how to alleviate the problems by using clever tactics. Furthermore, they know little about monitoring their own activities; that is, they do not think to plan, orchestrate, oversee, or revise their own learning efforts. (Brown, 1997: 400)

Similarly, other investigators were finding that the idea of strategies being taught through add-on courses was not as powerful as teachers and students enquiring into the process and experience of learning:

We do not foresee courses in metacognition being taught in schools. Rather we foresee that instruction in many areas of intellectual skill might be enriched by designing activities so that they bring more of the cognitive processes out into the open where teachers and students can examine and try to understand them. (Scardamalia and Bereiter, 1983: 62).

From the earliest studies, it has also been indicated that those approaches which promote reflection are more effective than those which promote skill-learning when it comes to 'results'. One programme used material from the history curriculum making it the object of reflection: another used generic learning skills materials. The students in the first group developed more advanced conceptions of learning, got better grades on essays and achieved better examination results (Martin and Ramsden, 1987).

So how are we to help pupils along this journey of learning about learning? A point which arises quickly in addressing that question is the need to develop a language for understanding one's learning. Here it will be clear that this is not a language of 'types' or 'styles': that is too limiting. Instead the focus we have adopted – learning about one's own lived experiences of learning – means that we will have to develop the language which humans have for talking with each other about their experiences: a narrative language, telling the stories of those experiences in an increasingly rich fashion. So here it may already be clear that the language for learning will not be provided by someone else, and it will not be in predetermined concepts: that would not honour the diversity to be found in effective learning.

Classroom practices for learning about learning have at their heart the practice of talking about experiences of learning and developing more sophisticated commentary about them. In earlier reviews of the literature (Watkins, 2001), the following four headings were derived to describe the practices:

- Noticing things about learning
- Talking about learning
- Reflecting on learning
- Planning and experimenting with learning.

These can be thought of in a cumulative sense, because in the context of the dominant picture of classrooms having little focus on learning the attention given to this area needs to be built up progressively.

First element: noticing learning

This requires that we occasionally *stop the flow* to notice our learning, bringing attention to the process of our learning. In this way we cumulatively build up a language for noticing learning. A range of prompts can help the first stage of noticing:

- What is learning? What do we mean? What is it not?
- When is it best? Where is it best?
- What helps your learning? (including, but not only, what teachers and others do)
- What steps or actions do you take in your learning?
- How did it feel?
- Does what you do and how it feels change as you go along?
- What surprises have you found?
- What hinders your learning?
- What do you learn for?
- What do you do with your learning?

Second element: conversations about learning

This starts with a range of prompts which help learners examine and discuss their experiences, so that they start to tell and re-tell stories of learning, with others, leading to dialogue.

- Tell me about a really good learning experience.
- What made it so good? What did you contribute?
- What does this tell you about you? About learning?
- How do you make sense of that?
- What puzzles you about that?
- What I notice in your story is …
- What differences do we see between our stories?

Third element: reflection

This can be supported through writing in a learning journal. As Lynne, aged 10, puts it: "As I write I notice and understand more too." A wide range of prompts can help to capture and review aspects of the learning journey, including those suggested by learners. Reflection is crucial for developing some distance from the immediate experience, and also may be supported by looking back over such records as are created through a learning journal:

- What was it like six months ago?
- What connections or patterns do you see?
- What new understandings about your learning have emerged?

Fourth element: making learning an object of learning

We may think of meta-learning as an additional cycle in the learning process (see Figure 9.1). Whatever the 'content' of our learning, we may achieve understanding through the Do-Review-Learn-Apply cycle which was developed in Chapter 6. We may also then focus on the process of learning we went through, as an additional cycle. In time this extra cycle becomes one which a learner can plan for, deciding which way they will go about their learning on this occasion and preparing to notice what happens in their experiment.

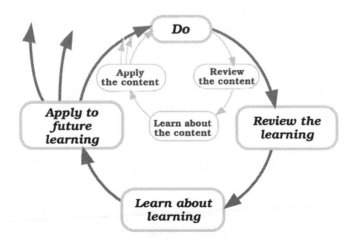

Figure 9.1 Meta-learning as an additional cycle in learning

Meta-cognitive knowledge about learning is constructed just like any other knowledge, pieced together on the basis of fragmentary data from a range of experiences. But it may then be used to turn learning into something we can experiment with and plan for.

- How can you plan to go about your learning?
- How can you monitor how your learning is going?
- How can you review how your learning has gone?
- To do a quality job on this project, we need to ...

With the use of the practices outlined above, any classroom can become more of a MOLE (Metacognitively-Oriented Learning Environment: Thomas, 2003) displaying these features:

In this classroom:

A Students are asked by the teacher to
- think about how they learn
- explain how they solve problems
- think about their difficulties in learning
- think about how they could become better learners
- try new ways of learning.

B Students discuss with each other
- how they learn
- how they think when they learn
- different ways of learning
- how well they are learning
- how they can improve their learning.

C Students discuss with the teacher
- as B above.

A Public Visible Presence in the Classroom

Conversations about learning are at the core of classroom practices and they can occur at many moments, sometimes brief and sometimes extended. But because of the fact that the wider environment does not support much dialogue on learning, this sort of talk can tend to die away unless it is maintained as a regular practice and supported by other practices in the classroom. Ensuring that the silence over learning does not return needs the creation of a public focus on learning in the classroom environment. Below are some examples of what we have seen in classrooms which are becoming learning-centred. The examples come from different years of primary schooling, as indicated after the teacher's name in each case, but they illustrate principles that could be applied in any year.

Public messages about learning (as opposed to work, perform, achieve):

"Are you getting on with your ~~work~~ learning?" (Joleene, Y 3)

Shared statements about our purposes in the classroom:

"To learn the best we can." (Sonia, Y 3)

Agreed principles for effective learning in the classroom:

"We need to question what we are told or what seems obvious or correct.
We need to feel that we have an equal chance to contribute/speak."
(Juliet, Y 6)

Reviews of when learning is best:

"A good classroom has sharing ideas and no-one left out." (Anna, Y 4)

Inquiries into learning, with learners' voices made public:

"I helped myself become engaged:
- When I heard you could make your own version of the story
- By knowing a short cut." (Sonia, Y 3)

Posters on themes and issues in learning:

"I love challenging activities because they make me think hard." (Zoe, Y 1)

"Mistakes are my friends: they help me learn." (Rebecca)

An explicit model of learning:

For example Do-Review-Learn-Apply.

Display of pupils' writing on their experiences and insights into their learning:

"Making up my own question helped me to think about what I really needed to know." (Simon)

Displays of 'work' with pupil commentaries on the learning associated with the products.

Evidence of Effects

There are two sources of evidence we want to refer to here. The first is that of classroom teachers who have been developing this area of practice, and gathering evidence of how learning is talked about in an enriched way. The second is that of researchers who have been surveying and investigating in this domain, and gathering evidence of the impact on understanding and performance.

Enriching pupils' views of learning

5 and 6 year-olds

Zoe (Bonnell, 2005) has been operating her classroom along some of the lines of a learning community, with public messages about learning, learning conversations and reviews. The effect of learning being a primary focus of everyday life is reflected in the writing from different children in the class after two and a half terms of learning about learning.

Pupils identify multiple learning resources in their environment

"I have learnt from books and the TV and even toys. I have learnt from fresh air. I have learnt from other people at class time. I have learnt from Mrs Bonnell. I have learnt from pictures and computers. I have learnt from writing." (Isabel, aged 6)

"We can learn by listening to other people. We can learn by reading books. We can learn by playing." (Aysha, aged 6)

"We learn from each other. We learn by listening. We learn from the teacher. We learn from books. We learn from looking at DVDs. Looking at the board. We learn from sitting on the carpet. We learn from looking at other people's work." (Annabel, aged 6)

Pupils mention social AND academic aspects of learning

"I have learnt how to make friends by asking them. I have learnt around the big table. I've learnt lots of hard maths." (Annie, aged 6)

"I've learnt that you can learn from other people. I've learnt that you have different ideas than other people … " (Ruth, aged 6)

Pupils talk about the empowerment of peer learning

"I have learnt more things because you [teacher] don't have to come round to all of the groups to tell us." (Lucy, aged 6)

Pupils start to identify their own learning goals

"I have learnt about numbers. I have learnt it by counting on the number square. I want to learn to read a book with small letters in it. I want to get better at cutting." (Sarita, aged 5)   (Bonnell, 2005: 64–5)

---

7 and 8 year-olds

Juliet spent time with her Year 3 class noticing learning, talking about how it feels, when it's best, and so on. After some time she asked them all to talk about the things that helped their learning. There were many 'ingredients' and the class then decided to put them into groups:

Doing	Feelings	Things	People
helping	past experience	fingers	brothers
sharing	energy	100 squares	friends
singing	support	information	other family
concentrating	safe	posters	sisters
focusing	patience	instructions	other children
talking	happy	books	parents
practising	encouragement	computers	doctors
listening	confidence	whiteboards	teachers
watching	comfortable	OHP	
writing	positivity	number lines	
quiet thinking	time	TV	
travelling		maps	
copying		labels	
co-operating			
reading			
playing			

What is noticeable here is the number of words for processes, and the great range of items. Posters with these words were displayed on the cupboard doors in the classroom, as a public support to the continuing dialogue, and were reviewed and developed at a later date.

10 and 11 year-olds

Naheeda (Maharasingam, 2004) has been holding conversations on learning with her Year 6 class for about a term. At the same time the class has been writing in learning journals, and the entries here seem to indicate a significant change over the period of a term:

Conceptions of learning in October

"You know that you have learned when something new is installed in your head."

"Learning is when you are educated by teachers."

"I think learning is when you don't know something and then you know it."

"I think learning is when you're learning something new."

"I see learning as acquiring facts. Sometimes it is mainly getting facts and making sense of them."

"Learning is when you listen to the teacher and store what she is trying to tell you."

Conceptions of learning in December

"Some people think learning is just stuffing information in your heads but it is not because the understanding is much more important. To be an effective learner you have to ask questions so you can challenge yourself instead of just sitting there and thinking you're perfect."

"I think responsible learners accept their mistakes and do their learning over and over again until they understand."

"When you ask questions you can learn more, but if you don't ask questions you stay in the same place that you were in."

"I think that you don't learn as well if the teachers just tell you because you can't just open your brain and pour in the information, you need to have had a full conversation about it."

A further reflection of this was pupils' responses to the prompt 'What's an effective learner'? By February, responses included:

"An effective learner wouldn't just know they will understand as well. They will feel motivated and never give up, they believe there is no such thing as I can't. If they get something wrong they will try again. If they don't understand they say."

"An effective learner asks questions. Even when they are really confused if they don't understand they say to themselves that they would try. They would believe it is how much effort they put in not how clever they are. They have a voice in their heads and believe in themselves." (pages 16, 17)

At the start children believed effective learners to be essentially passive but compliant: within a term effective learners are believed to be active, questioning, independent and confident.

12 and 13 year-olds

Emma (Williams, 2002) has spent time with secondary school students helping them notice, discuss and write about their experiences of learning. Many themes emerge in what they themselves report as the effects of this focus:

Learners make connections across contexts

"I found it really hard to put into words the 'how' of my learning in school, but it made me start to think when we talked about learning outside school. I love singing and I listen to learn most of my music – I'd never really thought about doing that when I am learning in school. For example I recorded all my exam notes onto tape and listen to them before bed. That has been really useful this term." (2002: 54)

"When I was learning to skateboard I kept doing small things again and again, until I really got them, and just looking at other people doing stuff and seeing what worked for them made me choose the next trick that I wanted to learn. There wasn't anyone telling me I should do this or that next, I just did what I thought was cool, and talked about my difficulties to friends, asking them what they thought about moves and things. I think that is really important to my learning – choosing the time to do something and choosing the way to do it. And being interested in the whole thing, I guess." (2002: 53).

Learners can take a perspective on their own feelings and previous strategies

"I can now see that I often avoid working hard because I think that if I don't do well, or if I fail an exam, I can sort of blame it on the fact that I didn't work. If I worked hard then I thought it would be really devastating if I failed but when I talked it through with John and Mark, I saw that they had that fear too – we actually decided it wouldn't be the end of the world, in fact we would probably do better if we worked hard, not worse." (2002: 77).

"I have learnt a lot about how my moods affect my ability to work – you often assume these things, but it's only when you start to write them down that you think, 'well I could do something about that'." (2002: 55).

Learners (in a high performing school) take a more balanced view of their achievements

"Learning is what I do as a human, to become a better human. How can exams test really important learning, like learning to love someone, or learning to cope when that person dies? I will try to stop beating myself up about not getting 'A' grades in exams because I think I have more to offer to the world than the sum total of my school exam results." (2002: 77).

15 and 16 year-olds

Shona (MacIntosh, 2005) has been operating her Year 11 English class as a learning community, with a strong focus on dialogue for learning and the class creating knowledge with and for each other. At the end of the year the group hold a reflective discussion on the process. Many themes emerge in the account, but some indicate that the pupils can now distinguish different approaches to supporting their learning·

Learners have a view of learning which is beyond techniques

Teacher: Is there overlap between the 'Learning to Learn workshop' that you've been doing with Mr X and our classroom as a learning community?

P1: I think the two concepts are different. With Mr X it's more learning *techniques* to learn, but what we do in English is learn about HOW we learn, so it's a kind of different concept.

P2: I think they're different in another way Mr X was telling me in a different conversation that the whole point of his workshop was to help us learn to improve our grades for our exams, but when you're going through it, I didn't think we were actually learning, it's more like how to cram revision into your head for an exam that's going to happen a few months or a few weeks or even days after the workshop. It wasn't learning it was more how to remember stuff … Why is someone doing it now when we could have been doing it for the last three years?

P3: I think that with us it's learning how we learn, and in the workshop it's telling us a '*good*' way to learn.

Learners are explicit about the role of reflection and relationships in a group

P3: I think before we had, I mean I'd certainly worked in groups before, but having never written down or had that help in the way I'd learned in that, I never sort of took that experience through to working in groups after that. So having written a reflective piece after the first group work we did this year, it has improved how we've worked as a group for the rest of the year I think. Whereas before we didn't have that chance in other classes

P6: I think that in English we work, we learn as a group, and with the 'Learning to Learn workshop' it's more individual learning. So if we use some of the techniques we've learned in the 'Learning to Learn' for say science, we would learn whatever it was we were trying to learn: in English, we would do this, y'know talk about it, our opinions, and write them down or whatever you like, and think about what other people are thinking, and learn from that. Learn from other people.

Learners describe how their view of learning has changed and helped with understanding and performance

P1: I don't necessarily think that in every English lesson every minute is spent as other teachers would call productively, but enabling them to do what I'm doing now, just babbling out loud. Have a chance, that opportunity, to do that as a whole group and as smaller groups means that I can clarify ideas in my head which in other subjects we're just not allowed to do.

P2: I think that as a class we were quite not bothered with the learning to learn when it started: I agree with that, and when we were debating issues most people had their heads down, fiddling with pencils and stuff, but as we learned that talking about the issue and debating our own ideas, we actually learned a lot more, and it also affected what we felt about these issues and it quite helped for when we actually did our essays. (MacIntosh 2005: video transcript)

To summarise, practices for learning about learning in classrooms can lead to changes in pupils' views of learning, in which we see evidence of progression through such features as:

- Greater independence from the teacher
- Greater number of sources for learning
- Self more in control of learning, seeing it as active, collaborative and learner–driven
- Learning seen more as a process and a journey which focus on meaning and understanding, rather than on techniques
- More ways of overcoming difficulties
- Learning seen more as a function of groups and communities
- Processes of clarifying and developing ideas through dialogue are emphasised
- Learning is seen as connected to "What I have to offer to the world."

In addition to this evidence of progression we see signs that learners themselves notice and mention their own progression in learning. Especially supported through learning journals, we find pupils who are able to comment on how their approach to learning now has moved on from what it was some time ago.

These features are not only the features of a more sophisticated or complex view of learning, they also have an empowering effect on learners whose extended repertoire and versatility can then be evidenced in 'results'.

Improvements in understanding and performance

The evidence from a range of research projects also shows significant effects of learning about learning on learners' understanding and performance. A more comprehensive review is available elsewhere (Watkins, 2001), and here we include a few examples through the years spent in school.

With 3 to 8 year-olds, experiments show that 'children who have been involved in this form of educational activity [including meta-learning] are better prepared for learning (understanding new content)'. Six year-olds showed greater understanding in three real-life learning experiments than did their peers (Pramling, 1990: 19).

For pupils aged 6 to 12 years, one programme which enhances children's strategies and meta-cognition helps them advance each others' understanding in small groups. Pupils are encouraged both to engage in self-reflective learning, and also act as researchers who are responsible to some extent for defining their own knowledge. The programme is successful at improving both literacy skills and subject knowledge. Rates of comprehension doubled, and ways of explaining became more connected (Brown and Campione, 1994).

Having learners pose meaning-oriented questions to themselves and to others, and having them exchange understandings, promotes high-level learning. Most effective questions are those posed by the learners themselves. Ten year-olds trained in this performed better in later learning tasks. Questions for linking with the learner's prior knowledge and experience and promoting connections to the lesson are more effective than questions simply designed to promote connections among ideas in a lesson: in this case 10 and 11 year-olds' performance on comprehension tests was greater (King, 1994). Thought-provoking questions (such as "Why is ... important?" and "What would happen if ...?") asked in small pupil groups elicit more explanations and in turn mediate learning: Year 6 pupils offered better explanations (King and Rosenshine, 1993).

Ten year-old pupils who learned about goals and strategies in learning sometimes improved their performance, but they also needed meta-learning in order to use the learning strategies (Kuhn and Pearsall, 1998). Learning about strategies and learning about learning go best hand-in-hand.

On transfer from primary to secondary school, when students view classrooms as having a learning orientation they have positive coping strategies and a positive feeling (Kaplan and Midgley, 1999). In secondary school, the more students are supported as autonomous learners the higher their school performance (Fortier et al., 1995). Better academic performance by 12 and 13 year-olds relates to a learning orientation and a malleable view of ability (Wolters et al., 1996).

Reviews of studies in the area of reading show that the teaching of meta-cognitive awareness, monitoring, and regulating has effects on performance 'among the larger ones that have been uncovered in educational research' (Haller et al., 1988: 7).

So at different ages in different contexts, a range of evidence supports the idea that a focus on learning leads to richer approaches to learning and in turn to improved performance. That's not the prime rationale for supporting learning about learning, but in these pressured times the evidence can help.

Voices Against Change

Here is an abbreviated sample of the sorts of things teachers tell us they hear – either in the voices of their colleagues, or in those voices in our own heads – which throw doubt on operating a classroom to support learning about learning. Alongside each we have put an equally abbreviated response voice. As you read them, think about how the balance of the voices is in your own context, and then do what you can to extend the answering voice in the right hand column:

"We've never done it before, so why start now?"	*Because the world has changed.*
"Our current practice works well enough."	*Only for some, and it could be better.*
"It's a luxury" (i.e. something we can't afford!)	*It's core, and we can't afford not to.*
"It'll end in tears – behaviour will get worse."	*Actually it gets better.*
"We need quick results."	*Results come in their own time.*
"It sounds like more work/more time."	*It is more time – on what matters.*
"Ofsted wouldn't like it."	*Have you checked that?*
"The pupils wouldn't like it."	*Try it and see.*
"I don't know much about learning."	*Fair point, but you can learn, alongside your pupils.*

There's a value in 'naming the game' with the voices in the left hand column, because they can become too powerful and stop us taking the first steps in inquiry, experimentation and change. Perhaps you will find a value in voicing the arguments which have been abbreviated in the right hand column. With practice at this you'll gain confidence about change.

Teachers Making the Change

Having seen many teachers create more learning about learning in their classrooms, there are some elements which seem to recur. These teachers:

- Realise that schools and classrooms have not been talking about learning.
- Have started to review their own learning experiences and learning history.
- Take the view that "it has to be better than this."
- Do not respond to the pressures for results by passing them on and being teacher-centred.

As they make their way along this journey, there are some other elements which can help to maintain progress:

- Obtaining sufficient practice, so that practices becoming ingrained in a classroom (after a start which had felt very much 'against the grain').
- Remembering to wonder about the process through which everyday learning takes place.

- Talking with their pupils about their own learning.
- Continuing to inquire into learning.

And what such teachers can also find is that despite the fact that their school context was not always the main agent in helping them start to innovate, others in the school may start to notice the positive effects and a ripple effect can begin to occur. When things start to move at school level, colleagues replicate the evidence from elsewhere: when teachers learn more about learning the effectiveness of a school improves and increased performance follows, especially for many of the underachieving students (Munro, 1999).

CHAPTER 10

Reclaiming Assessment to Promote Effective Learning

> *In this chapter*
> Exploring different conceptions of assessment
> How can assessment support effective learning?
> Classroom assessment strategies
> Assessment that is connected, embedded and authentic
> Making marking meaningful for learning

Throughout the book we have encountered the many ways in which too much of an unanalysed focus on assessment, especially assessment of performance, leads to distortions in classrooms: distortions of everybody's roles and of the purposes of school. And it does not lead to the achievements which the assessments were supposedly there to measure. So we will not be using this chapter to review the many things that are known about assessment in its widest sense: that would run the risk of reviving the distortion. Rather we aim to discuss the ways in which classroom assessment processes can support effective learning. So this chapter is a follow-up to the previous four chapters which have been outlining how classroom processes can support effective learning. We now add some classroom practices which might be called 'assessment'.

It is designed to help you consider:

- The relationship between effective learning in classrooms and assessment.
- How effective learning in classrooms can be supported and promoted through some assessment practices.
- What classroom practices you would like to include more of.

Exploring Different Conceptions of Assessment

There are many different, competing, overlapping and sometimes unexplored and unquestioned meanings that are associated with assessment. Some of these will support and promote effective learning, but some may even frustrate effective learning.

So we invite you to record your current responses to the prompt 'What is assessment?' (this is sometimes called 'brain-dumping'). Or if you are with a colleague, generate as many responses as possible to this prompt (sometimes called 'brain-storming').

A group of six teachers who we asked to do this exercise replied to the prompt 'What is assessment?' saying that it was:

- checking for learning
- diagnostic
- day to day
- minute by minute
- spontaneous
- validating learning
- testing out against criteria
- questioning
- formative and summative
- celebrating attainment.

How does this list compare with yours? Are there important differences? Are your responses more about processes of assessment or the products of assessment? And in the various purposes of assessment, whose interests are served? How much is it the case that young people's interests are served directly by the varied purposes, processes and products of assessment?

The results of this activity can also indicate some of the tensions and contradictions in assessment practices. In the list above we notice that there is no explicit link with supporting effective learning. This may reflect a lack of connection between assessment and learning in the dominant discourses and practices in our education system today (Hargreaves, 2005). Or it may reflect a particular connection, as Hargreaves' study showed, between a view of assessment-as-measurement and a view of learning-as-attaining-objectives. This connection is strong in policy discourses in England. But we also notice that our six teachers did not voice another discourse which is prevalent today, which is to use pupil performance assessment as a tool for judging the performance of a school. It is these discourses which lead many people in England to equate 'assessment' with 'tests'. School-wide performance testing, SATs (Standard Assessment Tasks) and the like cost billions of pounds and yet create unreliable results (Black, 2005). It makes English school students the most tested of all – nearly 100 public tests in a school career. By contrast, for many school students in Finland (a country which regularly tops the international comparisons) their first experience of a public examination is at the age of 16.

The systematic review mentioned in Chapter 4 (Harlen and Deakin-Crick, 2002) found strong evidence for the following impact of summative assessment and tests:

- a lowering of the self-esteem of less successful students which can reduce their effort and their image of themselves as learners
- a shift towards performance goals, rather than learning goals, which is associated with less active and less deep learning strategies
- the creation of test anxiety which differentially affects students
- judgements of value being made about students, by themselves and others, on the basis of achievements in tests rather than their wider personal attainment
- the restriction of their learning opportunities by teaching that is focused on what is tested and by teaching methods which favour particular approaches to learning.

Testing had the effect of hindering rather than supporting the learning of some and in some cases all students. The explanation for this illuminates again (but now in a negative sense) the main headings we have used in this book as the dimensions for promoting effective learning:

- being tested, especially in the controlled conditions of paper-and-pencil tests, is relatively passive, rather than involving active engagement with materials, ideas and people
- it is individualised not collaborative
- learner responsibility is not developed, it is something that is done to learners rather than driven by them, and it is designed by others for their own purposes
- meta-learning is not included, since testing elicits a narrow product of learning rather than the process of learning, and provides inadequate information for shaping strategies to improve learning (Darling-Hammond and Falk, 1997).

As noted in the research review above, the effect on learners and on their view of themselves and their experience of learning can be strong, and gives us good reason to find a better way. A study which asked pupils to draw their experiences of being tested found 'A large percentage of drawings portrayed students as anxious, angry, bored, pessimistic, or withdrawn from testing' (Wheelock et al., 2000). Some learners come to the view that they are no good, since they have identified themselves by relation to the test grade in the midst of many terms which focus only on test performance – "She's a C/D borderline"; "He's an 11+

failure"; "You're not as good as your sister." And in this situation of low agency for learners, others, like Hannah, fear losing their school identity:

> "I'm no good at spelling and [the class teacher] is giving us times tables tests every morning and I'm hopeless at times tables so I'm frightened I'll do the SATs and I'll be a nothing." (Reay and Wiliam, 1999: 345)

How Can Assessment Support Effective Learning?

If we are to reclaim the concept of assessment and build classroom practices which make a contribution to the promotion of effective learning, we need to reclaim the purpose of assessment. The origins of the term can give us a hint: it derives from the Latin *assidere* 'to sit beside', also reflected in the French *asseyer*. This could promote a constructive image of the teacher sitting alongside the pupil, especially in the educational context where the task is to bring out (in Latin *educere*) the learner's understanding.

As we move our focus from external testing which does not contribute to effective learning towards classroom assessment which does, two important shifts also occur:

- from a focus on what teachers do to a focus on what learners do
- from a focus on product and performance to a focus on the process of learning.

These moves reflect the themes of this book, but we also find them in what teachers say would be a better vision of what assessment could mean. Our group of six teachers above went on to produce the following set of provocative propositions: 'Assessment will support learning best when ...'

- the learner is assessing their own learning
- there are different forms
- the processes are understood
- learners make personal choices about how they demonstrate their learning
- it is continuous
- the learner understands its function
- it is an authentic experience
- the original meaning is reclaimed.

And in the bigger picture of things, such moves will be more easily achieved alongside a more informed vision of curriculum and learning. Lorrie Shepard (2000) summarised the connections in Figure 10.1.

Reformed Vision of Curriculum

- All students can learn
- Challenging subject matter aimed at higher order thinking and problem solving
- Equal opportunity for diverse learners
- Socialization into the discourse and practices of academic disciplines
- Authenticity in the relationship between learning in and out of school
- Fostering of important dispositions and habits of mind
- Enactment of democratic practices in a caring community

Cognitive and Constructivist Learning Theories

- Intellectual abilities are socially and culturally developed
- Learners construct knowledge and understandings within a social context
- New learning is shaped by prior knowledge and cultural perspectives
- Intelligent thought involves metacognition or self monitoring of learning and thinking
- Deep understanding is principled and supports transfer
- Cognitive performance depends on dispositions and personal identity

Classroom Assessment

- Challenging tasks to elicit higher order thinking
- Addresses learning processes as well as learning outcomes
- An on-going process, integrated with instruction
- Used formatively in support of student learning
- Expectations visible to students
- Students active in evaluating their own work
- Used to evaluate teaching as well as student learning

Figure 10.1 Shared principles of curriculum theories, psychological theories and assessment theory characterising an emergent, constructivist paradigm (Shepard, 2000)

Figure 10.1 aligns important values, understandings, approaches and practices across the three aspects of classrooms: learning theory, curriculum and assessment. It helps us understand the possibility of a positive relationship between the three. The learner is valued and the interests of the learner are put at the heart of each of the three aspects, including assessment. And it reminds us that learning and assessment also have a social and a meta-learning dimension. This fits with the view of effective learning developed in this book.

> Our aim now should be to change our cultural practices so that students and teachers look to assessment as a source of insight and help, instead of an occasion for meting out rewards and punishment. (Shepard, 2000: 10)

So if we are to make such a change, what might some of the classroom practices be?

Classroom Assessment Strategies

We offer here some examples organised under the same headings as the preceding four chapters. There might be a feeling that these overlap, which reflects their common aim of promoting effective learners.

Making classroom assessment active

Effective learning involves the learner actively engaging with materials, resources and ideas, and can be thought of in its key opening phases of 'Plan Do Review' (see Chapter 6). The same phases can be used with regard to engaging learners actively in assessment, so that learners plan how to assess (both process and product), do it, and also review how that assessment process went. These phases will help any learner come to greater understanding about assessment, at the same time as empowering their own thinking and evaluation. If the cycle continues to the point of actively applying such assessments, learners come to have more rich resources for improving their approach.

Classroom prompts which prepare the learner to actively assess can be used at the 'Plan' stage:

How will you tell whether the product you create is good?
How will you tell if the process you adopt is good?
How do you intend to do the best you can in this learning?

Learners' responses to these prompts may be traditional at first – that reflects their experience of school. But, as in all classroom tasks, engagement will develop as learners find their way, and start to propose richer assessment tasks that are performances of understanding based on higher order thinking. In the bureaucratically over-loaded classrooms of the UK, there has been an increased practice of teachers 'sharing' (i.e. telling) the 'success criteria' against which classroom performance is to be judged. These are distant and impersonal. The criteria through which any product is judged are less motivating if they remain someone else's criteria. Choosing how best to demonstrate understanding, and devising questions to check understanding, lead to depth and challenge. These also give students more control, make evaluation feel less punitive, and provide an important learning experience in itself.

If we are to make classroom assessment active in its use, then we need to consider what sort of judgements of performance can best lead to ideas for improvement. Clearly the sort of judgements which tests provide do not fit the bill here. They lead learners to devise rather empty strategies for improvement, sometimes with a compliant or moralistic style: "I'll try harder." This is because the process of learning and therefore of improving learning has not been highlighted. So learners need to be helped to develop a range of possible strategies, be prepared to try them out and to evaluate them. This is more likely to happen through peer discussion (see below).

Making assessment active can also happen in another sense, which is to inform it through active links to the world outside the classroom so learners could be supported in seeking evaluations of their products from people who might be adults in those disciplines, or potential users of their products. This helps classroom assessment to feel more like a consequential task: there is some real-life purpose to it, and indeed something could follow from it.

Making classroom assessment collaborative

As in many aspects of classroom life, much can be gained from distributing functions more widely (than loading them on an already overloaded teacher) by engaging peers in those functions. When it comes to assessment, peers can be very important in forming the bridge between the private and the public, that is between a learner's internal judgements (which can range from hesitant or unsure to extreme and negative) and a more validated and reality-based judgement. 'Feedback' is often talked about, but it must be something better than teachers again telling (Askew, 2000). Between peers processes of feedback can become a constructive exchange and levels of trust can be built up, as indicated in these comments from 6 year-old pupils when reviewing their practice of talking together:

> "In Talk Partners your partner can help you because they tell you different ways to work things out."
> "When my partner tells me how to do something in a better way, I know they are not being mean, they are just trying to help me." (Kurz, 2003: 46)

A key element in developing this is peer review of their discussions, so that learners come to handle their conversations in a helpful manner. The dialogue in such a review is exactly the same as is needed for high-level learning.

There are probably many peer-based assessment activities. When it comes to evaluating the process and product of one's activities, the point is that this could be profitably done with colleagues through using and adapting a range of devices. For example, in some UK classrooms the device of 'Traffic lights' is used, where learners use the green/amber/red of traffic lights to communicate some sort of assessment. In the hands of a performance oriented teacher, this device could offer them a quick performance check across the class on some low-level question – hardly a contribution to effective learning. But in other hands the device could be used to initiate a peer process which leads to rich learning talk (say pupils evaluating each other's explanations: see Black and Harrison, 2001). Many other such practices could be adapted similarly, along the lines of the principle of spreading them amongst peers.

The collaborative practices of peer-assessment also relate to 'self-assessment'. As noted in Chapter 8 students report that self- and peer-assessment makes them think and learn more (Stefani, 1994). The relation between peer-assessment and self-assessment centres on a quality dialogue. When this happens, the dialogue helps each individual to form a richer evaluation of their products and processes.

Making classroom assessment learner-driven

We now use the term 'self-assessment', but it is important to take care with this term: for some people it means them having to judge themselves (often their deficits) on someone else's criteria – hardly a contribution to effective learning. So we must build a better meaning for this term which encompasses learners developing the criteria, the methods for achieving them, and so on.

Even children of six years are able to participate in developing rubrics for their learning and also in applying criteria to the assessment of that learning. The quality of these rises over time (Higgins et al., 1994).

As the examples in Figure 10.2 indicate, when learners together specify the quality criteria for the product they are engaged in they use a wider range of personal criteria, yet incorporate those that would be given to them as 'success criteria'. Thus they make the success their own.

Year 4 – a written report

Year 8 – a collaborative concept map

"What is quality?"
  Neat – easy to read
  Proud of work
  Takes time
  Lot of self in work
  Thought it through
  Spelled right
  Used your skills
  Very interesting
  Good ideas
  Good thinking

"What is quality?"
  Focus question
  All ideas included
  Colour-coded
  Categories and groups
  Describes connections
  Legible and neat
  Correct spelling

Figure 10.2 Two examples of pupils' quality criteria

Helping pupils to plan how they go about their learning is a crucial development, even in a context where there are mandates, tests and so on. In Chapter 8 we described Susan, a language teacher, who encourages her students to design their learning to meet the requirement of mandated assessments. Her example highlights the importance of planning the means for how to achieve goals, even those set by others (Starnes and Paris, 2000). Susan's case probably gives us the most constructive version possible of 'teaching to the test' – a term which can mean different things in different classrooms (Smith, 1991) – and gives evidence of how maintaining a stance on effective learning will cope with these external forces. To some extent, it is possible to reclaim effective learning from other practices.

In the current UK context 'learning objectives' (i.e. performance objectives) which are 'shared with' (i.e. told to) learners can be reclaimed in a more active and learner-driven manner. Considerable engagement is evident when learners are asked to discuss with each other a provided learning objective using prompts:

- What could it mean?
- Who uses that?
- What might I be able to do with it?
- How could we best learn that?

As with peer-assessment, it is unlikely that there is a fixed list of strategies for self-assessment. Rather a range of devices could be adapted, and it is most impressive when we see learners themselves appropriating and adapting a device. Barbara, a deputy head, gave us the following example of a 10 year-old pupil when asked to identify the best example of self-assessment:

> A child in the class who experiences difficulty in writing, and had become quite demotivated, devised his own self-assessment record (smiley face) to record his feelings about his learning. I observed him doing this for a few days and then asked him about it. We talked about how it was helping him to remotivate and focus. He was also enjoying a new sense of achievement. He continues to make good progress.

This brief example not only illustrates the pupil appropriating a monitoring device which the class had used for feelings and adapting it to learning, but also gives a brief account of the connections between his greater awareness, control, and improvement.

Making classroom assessment into learning about learning

Making learning explicit is a key part of effective learning, so when we consider assessment we need to find ways in which learners can evaluate and develop their learning. Here again the term 'self-assessment' arises, but we must use it to mean assessment of oneself (not merely by oneself), especially of oneself as a learner. In one example, 12 year-old students devised four 'levels of excellence' on which they regularly rated themselves in a number of their current areas of activity (Table 10.1). The terms which these students used carry an engaging sense of what it means to increase expertise in something, including the way in which one's relationships develop.

Table 10.1 Four levels of assessing oneself as a learner

	Teaching/learning role
Novice	Needs help or direction
Apprentice	Learns with some assistance
Practitioner	Functions independently
Scholar	Facilitates learning

Importantly, learners can regard themselves as novices in one area and scholars in another. Some examples of how they talk about themselves in this process suggest that it engages a powerful sense of themselves as advancing: "I have risen up from ... to ...", "You evaluate how you have grown", and so on.

The longer-term development of oneself as a learner is often supported with a learning journal. When we travel on a journey we might take a journal, to note the places on our way and build up an overall picture of the expedition. This is so with learning. Journals often begin as a record of the learning experience, but the act of writing helps the learner to stand back and see more. So the meta-level is promoted by aspects of evaluation. It is an example of noticing learning. As mentioned in the previous chapter, the journal allows the writer to objectify. One 10 year-old wrote to her teacher "I see that as I write log entries I tend to read them ... These log entries help me a lot. As I write I notice and understand more too" (Sanford, 1988).

Learning journals take energy to initiate, but we have found that sentence starters or prompts can help the learner begin. Some examples to get started are:

I am proud of my learning today because I ...
One thing I am learning about myself as a learner is ...
Today I made an important breakthrough in my learning. The thing that helped me was ...

The meta-level can be promoted when a second entry is made that comments on an original entry to illuminate the learning processes. Some examples at the meta-level would be:

I notice that over time I have …

I think I'm making progress as a learner because …

I am noticing that I am becoming more of a strategic learner because I …

Students need continuing experience to become fluent in assessing their own learning. The skills that students need to grasp can be promoted through a range of everyday activities and strategies, such as those in Table 10.2.

Table 10.2 Developing skills of assessment

Skills and knowledge for learners to develop	Strategies to develop these skills
Awareness of self as learner: looking at oneself from a distance and developing a view of self as learner	Talk about learning Reflection (e.g. through learning journal) Review of learning journey (e.g. in portfolios) Peer appreciation Photographs of the learner activity for stimulus "I can …" sheets (e.g. recording achievement) Teacher feedback
Understanding of learning purposes	Talking about learning intentions Setting own learning intentions (i.e. not teaching intentions) Learning (not performance) goals Checking with a peer

Knowledge of strategies to achieve intentions	Talk with peers and teachers
	Public resources: e.g.
	    lists of words for learning processes
	    strategy lists

Evaluation skills, such as comparison, evaluating strategies, feelings, outcomes, etc	Creating quality criteria Frameworks: e.g. "I can" sheets, smiley faces, traffic lights Listening to teacher or peers evaluating
Learning to use the language to talk about this	Talking about strategies, feelings, purposes, context, effects Learning journal and portfolio prompts Developing narrative with teachers and peers Listening, responding and questioning skills for creating a dialogue

In many of the activities and strategies described above the processes of assessment can be integrated into the learning activities, not added on as a separate activity. In this way classroom assessment becomes a very different process from testing, and the long-term goal would be to operate classrooms which in their support of effective learners also supports an embedded process for learners to notice, evaluate and improve on their processes and products.

Assessment that is Connected, Embedded and Authentic

As Shepard suggested in Figure 10.1, rather than keep assessment separate from learning and the curriculum, learners can be supported to evaluate both the content of their learning and the process by the approach underpinning the curriculum. At Mission Hill School in Boston in the USA the students are encouraged to learn using the framework of five key questions as in Table 10.3.

Table 10.3 The 'habits of mind' framework (Costa and Kallick, 2000)

Habits of mind	Concerned with ...
What do I see/hear/touch/feel/smell?	Evidence
Who says?	Point of view
What does this remind me of?	Connections
What if ...? How else ...?	Conjecture
Why does it matter?	Relevance

During a visit to the school one of us noticed 6 and 7 year-old students discussing the then current presidential elections and the qualities needed to become president. One question posed was "Do they call it the White House because it's only for white people?" Another was "Does the president get tired of being the president?" These questions reflect critical and empathic standpoint-taking, which are crucial habits of mind. In this school the young people are assessed by portfolio, presented to a committee of adults, and observed by younger students. The habits of mind reflect a desire for the learning of the young people to be authentic, which the co-principal described as the intention of "getting the student into the adult world." These same five questions could be adapted to promote reflection on the students' own learning.

Another key aspect of assessment that supports learning appears to be including more real-world or authentic tasks. This implies a broad range of performances: oral presentations, collections of written and other products, solutions to problems, records of experiments, debates, research projects by individuals and groups, teacher observations and portfolios of students' work and learning (Darling-Hammond and Falk, 1997).

The use of portfolios can also contribute to more connected learning, since the element which is a record over time can support another element which is the student commentary. As a learner comes to be explicit about what the evidence they have gathered shows in relation to learning, and the way in which the learning is developing, the portfolio can be used to help the understanding of learning. In other words, to use portfolios effectively to support learning requires a shift in emphasis to the analysis and integration of learning rather than merely a collection of evidence. An account of the learning that has taken place can be stimulated by prompts for reflection:

What do earlier entries tell you about your learning at that point?
In what ways can you see the entries changing?

Research has suggested that three things are important to help portfolios be more than a collection of 'best work' (Klenowski et al., 2006).

* Establishing the purpose of the portfolio with learners
* Noticing the effects of the portfolio on learning
* Planning changes in the approach to learning as a result of reflection on the portfolio contents and process.

One finding from research into the use of portfolios in this way was that the learners took ownership of their learning in different ways (Klenowski et al., 2006). The researchers also found that this approach represented a view of learning in which the learner explicitly constructs their learning rather than seeing it as something that is dictated externally. It is important that the learner has this constructivist view of learning and the teacher needs to be explicit about the approach to learning on which the portfolio is based.

Making Marking Meaningful for Learning

Marking of students' work can be a major chore and burden for teachers, with relentless expectations from others making it feel like an endless hamster wheel. We question the purpose of this activity, especially when we consider the words used to describe it, such as 'marking' (What are the marks – grades or notations?). 'Correcting' is an associated term, but teachers correcting students' products are unlikely to support the learning in any meaningful way: knowing what was wrong does not necessarily mean that you now know what is right or how to make it so. 'Grading' is another term, which focuses on the evaluative aspect of the activity, often as an activity at the end of a unit. Paying attention to the students' efforts can be an important feature of marking, but with little review of how that might promote learning. The witnessing aspect of marking could be achieved with much less time and effort by the teacher.

Many teachers will share Nicki's concern as a teacher, that she was spending a great deal of time 'marking' her students' work, and yet had very little idea about how it helped them improve their learning, or indeed whether it did help their learning at all (Charles, 2004).

She was impressed by the idea of focused marking (Clarke, 2001) and decided to undertake some action research around its introduction. Focused marking encourages communication between learner and teacher indicating successes, improvement related to the lesson focus, suggestions for improvement and providing time for the improvement to be made. It also suggests that only a selection of learners' 'output' should be marked. Nicki used a class of 8 year-olds, and assessed their states of learning before, during and after the implementation of this form of marking. She used imaginative methods (questionnaires and scenarios) to assess whether their responses indicated they were one of the four states as shown in Figure 10.3 (attributed to Robinson, 1974).

	Unconscious	*Conscious*
	(of a need to learn a specific skill or knowledge)	
Incompetent	Unconscious incompetence	Conscious incompetence
Competent (relative to a specific skill or knowledge)	Unconscious competence	Conscious competence

Figure 10.3 Four possible states of the learner

She found evidence that these young people had increased their awareness of their learning, and were able to be more explicit themselves about this.

> "You can use Mr Curry's comment that he's written in your book to start working on it, thinking … Shall I write a different answer? Or shall I answer Mr Curry's comment?" (Henry)
>
> "Sometimes I feel rushed because we only get like five minutes to write, and you know that you want to write a lot of feedback." (Amelia)
>
> "It tells us a bit more about our learning." (Roma)

Nicki contrasted these comments to one made to her earlier

> "Miss, all that matters is that you're getting the right answer, right?" (Charles, 2004)

We like this example because Nicki was checking whether her students were able to change their learning practices as a result of her marking. She wanted them to become more aware or conscious of themselves as learners, and of what they were doing.

Concluding Thoughts

This chapter on reclaiming assessment happens to come at the end of a sequence of chapters on promoting effective learning in classrooms, but the messages in it have been similar and relate to all of the chapters which have preceded it. They may be summarised as follows:

- The situation is powerful
- Learning is local
- Change is local.

So the message of this particular chapter is that assessment should not be dominated by the presence of national testing systems of a narrow nature, of dubious reliability, and of phenomenal cost in both financial and psychological terms. There are plenty of rich alternatives which this chapter has tried to briefly indicate. Are any of them offering new possibilities for practice in your classroom?

Further, in response to the evidence that what teachers do in their classrooms is the most powerful element of the system, we should continue to strive towards what learning-enriched schools do. They are not compliant places and can find themselves doing things which are often 'against the grain' of the pressures which undoubtedly try to influence them. And at best they manage to embed their local solutions into the culture of their schools, so that which was 'against the grain' manages to become 'engrained' in everyday practice. Some of the dynamics surrounding that are addressed in the next chapter.

PART III

THE FUTURE IN CONTEXT

Being Exceptional

The point of this chapter is:

- To emphasise that there are many exceptional teachers and classrooms – in two senses: (1) they are inspiring and promote effective learning, and (2) they are an exception to the dominant way of talking about and being in classrooms.
- To think about classroom change in that light, especially change which is 'against the grain'.
- To help those who may have read this book reasonably completely to review where they have reached.
- To anticipate some issues in helping you extend your contribution to the creation of exceptional classrooms.

Learning from the Best of your Past

At the start of this book we invited you to undertake an appreciative inquiry, for which the focus lay with classrooms you had known where the learning had been really positive. Our experience of doing this inquiry with many teachers is that the results relate well with our main headings for promoting effective learning in classrooms (Chapters 6 to 9). We hope that this was the case for you, and that this book has affirmed and extended your view of classroom practices.

We now want to consider the process of change in classrooms and ask you to undertake another appreciative inquiry, but this time the focus is not on a classroom you have known: it is your own experience of changing classrooms. Our idea is that every reader will have had experiences when they themselves were exceptional, when they handled something in a classroom in a way which did not replicate the dominant model. We want to learn from that, and take into the future the best of our past.

Take a few minutes to think about an occasion when you deliberately handled something about your classroom in a different way. Perhaps it was the activity, your role, the social structure, and so on, but you tried to create a difference that made a difference. Choose the best experience you can.

When you have identified the situation do all you can to reconstruct it in your mind's eye – recall the occasion, the conditions, the people and so on. Capture the concrete details of the change that you made, as well as the things that led you to try something new on this occasion. If possible, share this with someone else.

Now we want to learn about two aspects of that occasion: the content of your change, and how you managed to do something different from the dominant model.

The first part of this inquiry is about the details of your change.

What was the new thing that you tried out? Was it a new activity, a new way of handling your role, a new way of structuring the class, a new conversation or inquiry … ?

What was the theme that you now see in the change you made?

- Was it a different view of a classroom activity?
- Or a way to have learners help each other?
- Or a way that they set the agenda?
- Or a way to allow a focus on learning?
- Or something else entirely?

What was it about the change you made which made it different from the dominant teacher-centred classroom?

You can probably imagine that there are many detailed accounts of changes that teachers make, and they come back to life with this inquiry. But there are also some large effects described in these stories, especially when they capture the idea of a focus on learning. On these occasions we hear teachers saying such things as "My relationships have changed – much better now" and "I feel a lot better about being a teacher." Our view is that the shift to a focus on learning has the sort of effect which we hear talked about but less often evidenced: an apparently small intervention leading to a large change. So it is something about the system of the classroom which is altered here, and Weimer (2002) summarised some of the changes when teaching is learner-centered as:

- The balance of power
- The function of content
- The role of the teacher
- The responsibility for learning
- The purpose and process of evaluation.

Often the examples we hear about have somehow managed to stop the flow of a teacher-centred classroom, so that some more openness and new possibilities can enter.

The second part of the inquiry is about how you managed to do something exceptional.

- Where did you get the idea for the change you made? What sources were important?
- Once you had got the idea, what were the voices against you doing it? And how did you handle those voices?
- In what other ways did you help yourself?
- What resources do you have from your history, heritage, family and other experiences which help you to do exceptional things that make a difference?
- What else helped?

There are so many important things that can come to light during this activity. Here are some very brief snippets from stories we have heard:

I was bored and so were the kids.
I had this idea on the train.
I had become a spoon-feeder.
I remembered someone saying that the biggest risk in education is not to take one.
We've seen more pilots than British Airways but no real change.
There are quite a few nonconformists in my family.
My mother would have been proud.

For a more extended example, we asked Mike Hughes (author of a classroom experiment we considered in Chapter 8 – see Hughes 1993, and also Hughes

1997 and 2002) to tell us how he managed to run his classroom 'against the grain'. He gave this analysis:

External factors
- A 'Flexible Learning Project' provided some limited but welcome additional funds.
- The style of GCSEs (with a significant component being coursework).

Internal factors
Supportive headteacher (never raised an eyebrow at whatever I suggested! I knew/felt that he had complete confidence).

Personal/professional factors
There is no doubt in my mind that the most significant factor was my own views about Teaching and Learning. Internal/external factors simply created the context – in some ways they helped (i.e. supportive head), in some ways they made it more difficult (many said the National Curriculum would put an end to all this 'trendy stuff').

I would have done this in my classroom (or something very similar) regardless of context because of:
- A rejection during my early years of teaching as the 'transfer of information, students write it down and get a red tick' mode of teaching that I saw in many classrooms.
- A personal/professional opinion that 'There has to be more to it than this'.
- A deep conviction that children need to enjoy learning, have fun, be engaged in the process and treated like adults (or more accurately with respect!): relationships are key to the classroom, etc.

What strikes us about this account includes:

Mike found support for unorthodox ideas – he didn't make himself into a martyr

Extra resources (such as money) can be handy but are not essential

Mike was aware of the forces operating in his context

He had a core set of beliefs about learners and learning

There is a key phrase here: 'There has to be more to it than this'.

On a much wider scale, it seems that many teachers in England have experiences which echo those here. A survey of a representative sample of 10,000 teachers in England (GTCE, 2004) asked the question 'Thinking about the most effective and inspirational lessons you have ever taught, what were the main sources for your ideas?' The top three answers were:

Interactions with pupils (79 per cent)

Reflecting (78 per cent)

Talking with colleagues (61 per cent)

These are important findings for the stance we take: change is local. And they also emphasise the crucial role of a teacher's own thinking and their ideas for making things better. So what is your vision for classrooms of tomorrow?

Looking Ahead: Your Vision for Classrooms in the Future

At the start of this book we invited you to create some 'provocative propositions' about when learning is best in classrooms. This activity was intended to provoke your thinking into creating more of the best in your classroom by envisioning what it might look like and how it could come about. Look back at your responses to this activity: notice what you felt then and compare it with how you would react now, having read more of this book.

Being exceptional can be a challenge, but handling it is helped by clarifying your vision of your classroom. Perhaps provoked by reading Chapters 5 to 10, what do you want to see developed in your classroom? What have you taken from your reading of this book or other sources?

And what are your thoughts about the bigger picture? How do you think classrooms should be in a decade's time – or longer than that? Recently, the Organisation for Economic Co-operation and Development (OECD, 2001b) asked experts from the USA, Australia and five European countries (but not the UK) 'What Schools for the Future?' Their report painted a picture of six possible scenarios, with two of each under three major themes:

The status quo extrapolated

1 Robust bureaucratic school systems

2 Extending the market model

The re-schooling scenarios

3 Schools as core social centres

4 Schools as focused learning organisations

The de-schooling scenarios

5 Learner networks and the network society

6 Teacher exodus – the 'meltdown' scenario   (OECD, 2001b)

Some of the scenarios that teachers would not want are well indicated in these brief phrases. And the scenarios which educators did choose (3 and 4) have community and learning as their key contributions. Does this accord with your broad view?

At the classroom level, there are parallels: we do not wish classrooms to become more like teaching machines, or qualifications shops, or test-prep factories. Rather we seek a combined focus on social and learning processes. It is also worth noting that the idea for schools of the future does not imply that classrooms will disappear or become rows of computer terminals.

How might you express your vision for your classroom to yourself? And how might you express it to your colleagues or your students or their parents? Many teachers feel silenced within their staffrooms in expressing ideas about richer forms of learning. One of the themes of this book is to encourage teachers to reclaim and celebrate their professional voices in classrooms and staffrooms, to do this collaboratively, and to keep it public.

Issues in Thinking about Changing Classrooms

Having thought ahead, let us consider the issues in getting there. Throughout the book we have included accounts of some of the teachers we have worked with (and there are plenty more) who have made their classrooms into exceptional places. Their investigations and experiments to promote effective learning in the classroom have involved young people in being active, learning collaboratively, being responsible for their learning, and learning about their learning. Others have investigated young people's conceptions of learning, which also starts the process of young people noticing their learning, gaining insights into their various learning processes and leading to make their learning more effective. While some of their changes may seem small, the results were dramatic and even profound. The investigations led to further experiments and had important effects on other teachers in their schools. Shifts can be huge because as the focus moves to young people's learning teachers and young people take new and different learning roles.

Teachers we know who have been exceptional have distilled some of their experience into advice for their colleagues, and we have reviewed the advice with others. Their thoughts on creating and sustaining change to bring about richer learning in classrooms are summarised in Table 11.1 and we comment on them below.

Collaborate

Teachers suggest it is more exciting and more sustaining, and innovations are better supported when they work alongside other teachers. This may be within the school, building strategic alliances with other teachers, or on courses or

Table 11.1 Issues in making changes in classrooms

Collaborate	With other members of staff
	With young people
	With colleagues outside school
	With colleagues in professional dialogue about learning
Be rigorous	Focus on learning, don't slip into teaching
	Notice, share and record or collect evidence
	Analyse your findings, successes and other outcomes
	Scrutinise your findings against research
	Consider the implications for the curriculum and assessment
	Keep it public
Be flexible	Be patient: investigation takes time
	Findings may be ambiguous/uncertain/ inconclusive/contradictory
	Innovate
	Find and create opportunities for change
	Expect the unexpected
	Don't over-plan
	Take what may feel like a risk
and …	Start with what concerns you
	Search for other resources e.g. via the internet
	Remember that there are always relational and affective aspects of change

projects involving colleagues from outside the school. It is harder to be and to remain exceptional on your own. Collaboration allows teachers to hear new ideas, deal with doubt and uncertainty, and talk through and understand change (Carnell, 2001). Many teachers have used collaborative occasions to discuss what they have been reading and to develop their understanding of the experiences and ideas of others about learning in the classroom. The most frequently used descriptor of such groups is 'excitement'.

The involvement of young people is similarly important. This is not simply gathering information in surveys or interviews, but actively making meaning about learning with the teachers. Once young people become involved in the investigations or changes they initiate further developments themselves. On occasions when a change was not working well in the classroom, the children were able to help the teacher resolve the issues. The key to this involvement is dialogue between young people and with teachers about learning (Lodge, 2005; Fielding, 2004).

Be rigorous

When we ask teachers to focus on learning it takes a little while for them not to default to a focus on teaching. The focus on learning is what really makes the difference. It pays to attend to the language being used (e.g. learning not work). Keeping the changes and investigation public in the life of the classroom also helps maintain the focus on learning.

The development of ideas and frameworks against which to scrutinise findings from their own classrooms is where collaborative reading adds an important dimension to the rigour. Evidence can be noticed, shared and collected in uncomplicated ways. Many different forms have been used: drawings, comments, products, videos, surveys and feedback from reviews, as well as assessment data. Making sense of the evidence, can be helped by the Do-Review-Learn-Apply model. The participation of young people in making sense of the evidence can add an extra dimension and help teachers avoid pitfalls such as romanticising, homogenising or ignoring some aspects of what is before them. Writing reports or assignments for courses and for colleagues, especially collaborative writing, is important and is much more engaging and enjoyable than teachers at first predict.

Be flexible

This involves recognising the social realities of school and the dynamic nature of learning and teaching. Investigations and experiments to support richer forms of learning will not necessarily proceed in a linear way or indeed as you intended. Sometimes you may need to seize an opportunity that you had not anticipated. On other occasions the reactions to your small changes, for example, may produce such interesting effects that you need to take time to consider and understand them. We have often observed that teachers start by investigating one thing and as a result get enthusiastic and excited by something connected to it, and develop their focus as a result.

Time is a highly prized resource for teachers, but working collaboratively often results in more productive work in less time – and is also more enjoyable. Investigation into learning is best sustained over time, it is not an instant fix. Nor is it the sort of investigation where teachers put on a white coat, pick up a clip-board and mimic the stereotype of a scientist, 'proving' things with samples and control groups and so on. The work of learning and teaching will always contain ambiguity, so it helps not to look for certainty. Perhaps better to remember the words of Albert Einstein: "If we knew what we were doing, we wouldn't call it research."

Being exceptional can change more things than the learning in a classroom. It can affect people's relationships with each other (young people with each other, and with teachers, and teachers with other teachers) and the emotions of young people and teachers. A consistent outcome of our project work with teachers has been the levels of enthusiasm and excitement at engaging in this kind of activity. At the start young people can be less enthusiastic: they may be suspicious, anxious about what it will mean for them because they may be required to respond differently, they can believe that this will not help results, and so on. More often they respond with enthusiasm of a mature sort, like the 13 year-old with a big reputation for bad behaviour in a London comprehensive, who said to Gemma (his science teacher) after a few sessions of operating as a learning community "Miss, it's been good doing it this way, and y'know, it's about time." For that same class Gemma's comment expressed something we have heard before: "They learned a lot more than they were meant to!"

In that example it would be hard to say that Gemma found herself in a supportive environment for her experiments: the vast majority of colleagues in the school knew nothing about them, and the overall climate of the school was not particularly supportive. But a small group of colleagues were working on this theme together, and that brings us to consider how to think about change in such circumstances. We are regularly asked by teachers whether they can make change when their school context is not supportive: our answer is "Yes." Of course it is less easy to do this on one's own, but it is possible. And it re-emphasises a point made above: that some sort of network of support, either inside or outside your school, can be very important.

Try mapping out the people in your school and any contacts who you think would make helpful strategic alliances for supporting inquiries and experiments into developing more effective learning in your classroom.

And now we offer some thoughts which are about the same theme at a larger level: how we consider creating change when an education system is not supportive. We have already seen some examples in Chapter 5 of teachers working 'against the grain' of the dominant culture, and we wish to add our own learning about that in the hope that it will help you to remain exceptional.

Working Against the Grain – What Have We Learned?

We first started to use the phrase 'against the grain' in 1995, when reviewing the aftermath of the first national curriculum in England. The purpose of the term was not to be counter-cultural or subversive – that would have been a misdirection of energies, organised around the wrong values – but to be open-handed about the fact that we were moving in a different direction to the dominant trend and the official voices. The term had value in helping honour our experience and evidence. Three aspects of what we have learned since that time will be mentioned here: the focus on learning, the focus on the classroom, and 'naming the elephant'.

The first thing we had to learn was how difficult it is to focus on learning, the supposed centre of what school is for. The language is under-developed, and there are many aspects of our everyday discourse which take us away from a focus on learning. Exacerbated by the policy context of the last 18 years, the tendency is to talk about (i) teaching, (ii) performance, and (iii) work. It has been useful to identify these three 'space invaders', so that we can notice the ways they take up the space we would wish to give to a focus on learning (Watkins, 2003). We may not vanquish the space invaders, but our task is to tame their negative influence on our professional vision and practice. As we outlined in Chapter 4 and elsewhere, the performance discourse distorts the purpose of education and leads to many forms of strategic behaviour: putting effort into limited goals, giving up when things get tough, aiming to 'look good' rather than to learn, and to adopt any strategy that might get a better showing in performance measures. Nowadays evidence of the systemic effects are more widely known, including 'administrator and teacher cheating, student cheating, exclusion of low-performance students from testing, misrepresentation of student dropout rates' and so on (Nichols and Berliner, 2005).

The second point was to focus on the classroom, for again there are many forces in the current environment which take our attention away from the detail of the classroom and on to policies and systems and management and paperwork and targets and compliance. These have the effect of emphasising hierarchy, but the evidence shows that hierarchical forces are not all-powerful. The variation between schools and between classrooms makes this point:

> Recent research on the impact of schools on student learning leads to the conclusion that 8–19% of the variation in student learning outcomes lies between schools with a further amount of up to 55% of the variation in individual learning outcomes between classrooms within schools. (Cuttance, 1998: 1158)

So the classroom is the influential context, and the hazard is that top-down management can reduce participants' capacity to self-organise (Olson, 2003) which is a crucial capacity in being an effective learner. And it can also reduce the agency which is a hallmark of expert teachers (Berliner, 2001). So our task becomes one of bringing to the surface teachers' knowledge of learners and learning which has become submerged below the rhetoric of compliance and managerialism. The practices of appreciative inquiry which are evident in this book contribute greatly here.

A third element was needed to understand some hesitation amongst teachers to experiment with learning in their classrooms, and here the idea of 'naming the elephant' was useful. It refers to a group of people talking in a room where there is also an elephant – but no-one mentions it. In the UK's education system, the elephant that people do not mention is fear, and it deserves to be named so that its effect may be analysed and tamed (Hammond and Mayfield,

2004). Otherwise we will continue with a climate of poor communication which can have disastrous consequences. Narrative work helps us see that the voice of fear does its life-negating work through exaggeration – over-stating each of the likelihoods of "You'll get caught" and "It will be dreadful" (Wagner and Watkins, 2005). On closer inspection, most teachers find that neither of these occur much, which confirms the evidence that 90 per cent of human fears do not eventuate (Jeffers, 1997). But the climate of bullying has created fear and if teachers are to regain professional confidence (the ability to continue acting according to your principles while in the presence of the voice of fear) a better direction needs to be found. This is also likely to reclaim moral and ethical standards at a time when market forces have unprecedented power, and return the teaching profession from its current misaligned state (Gardner et al., 2001).

So the elements of focusing on learning and focusing on the classroom emphasise that the powerful context for learning and change is the local setting, and they help us to maintain a skeptical view of any account of the education system which portrays it as a single story to which it is our duty to comply. The evidence does not support such an account. The elements also emphasise that going to the root of our education system – learning and classrooms – is the act of the activist professional (Sachs, 2000) who can be described in both senses as a 'learning teacher'.

Do these themes add to your possibilities of working against the grain? Teachers currently seem to be surrounded by invitations to comply with someone else's ideas: how have you managed to decline such invitations? There are also times when we may be recruited into practices we disagree with: how have you managed to minimise any negative effects of this?

Making a Change – The Content

When we look ahead to making a change that will make a difference for learning in classrooms, it's possible to look ahead to two aspects: the 'what' and the 'how'. Choosing the 'what' may come from a range of sources – interactions with pupils, your own vision, conversations with colleagues, a story, a course or a book. There's certainly no one best place to start given the complexity of the classroom. But sometimes that complexity leads us to not start at all, so the little device on page 170 is offered as a help to you choosing a starting point.

Choose a classroom where you feel like you would like to be involved in promoting more effective learning. Think of the current profile of activities for pupils in this classroom.

On the scale below give a quick indication of the extent to which the profile of activities in the classroom could be described by each of the headings.

	Very little	Somewhat	Quite a lot	A lot
Active Learning	☐	☐	☐	☐
Collaborative Learning	☐	☐	☐	☐
Learner-driven Learning	☐	☐	☐	☐
Learner about Learning	☐	☐	☐	☐

(a) Which of the four would you choose as priorities for development in this classroom?

(b) Which of the four do you think you are likely to make experiments with?

Now think ahead in some more detail: the task design, activity, participant structure, and so on. Then remember that this is an experiment designed to make a difference, so you wouldn't want to miss the difference it makes – you may well have to prepare yourself for that.

Making a Change – The Process

Planning change seems like an oxymoron at times, especially when we hear people in this field saying that you can't mandate what matters. So remembering teacher advice about not over-planning, the most appropriate thing we can offer you is a few reminders of some of the themes in this chapter:

- Will your experiment/inquiry be you alone, you with a colleague in the same classroom, you coordinating with colleagues in other classrooms?
- Can you anticipate anything which could hinder your plan? And pre-empt it? And building on what you know from successful examples, what might help it? And how can you engage that?
- Will you engage pupils in the plan from the start (e.g. by inviting their voice on the issue you have chosen)?
  If not, how will you present the experiment in such a way that it is likely to engage them?
- Which class will you choose for this experiment?
  Are you choosing an appropriate level of risk for valuable learning to follow?

- How many sessions with the class will your experiment take?
  When will you do any detailed planning/replanning of the tasks/activities/...?
- What will you be looking for in order to learn more about this experiment?
  What will you intend to notice while the experiment is underway?
  How will you collect the learners' views during and after?
- Who will you talk with about what you notice?

And in order that you are not completely put off when you take new steps against the grain, why not ask: How will you handle your relapses to a teacher-centred practice? They may well happen but may also be overcome.

Effective Learning for Teachers

Finally, we wish to entertain a connection between the major categories we have used in this book for promoting effective learning in classrooms on the one hand, and teachers' learning on the other hand. These two rarely get discussed in the same terms because there seems to be a view that young people's learning has to be thought of as in some different way to that of adults (we do not find supportive evidence for that view). Sadly we hear stories that teachers are treated to experiences which do bear some similarity to the experiences of pupils in classrooms: they are talked at, on someone else's agenda, expected to comply and judged afterwards. This is what teachers' in-service training has become on too many occasions.

Instead, the connection we wish to entertain is that the best examples of teachers' learning are occasions characterised by the very same things as characterise effective learning for pupils:

- Active learning
- Collaborative learning
- Learner-driven learning
- About learning.

We can imagine a whole new range of enquiries into that, but will keep that for another time. The more we do have those qualities in classroom learning and teacher learning, the more it is likely to be the case that we can all be exceptional.

References

A Correspondent (1959) 'Strangers in the classroom: a master's reactions to teaching under observation', *The Times*, (31 March): 10.

Abbott, Martin L. and Fouts, Jeffrey T. (2003) *Constructivist Teaching and Student Achievement: The Results of a School-level Classroom Observation Study in Washington*. Washington: Seattle Pacific University, Washington School Research Center.

Alderson, Priscilla (2003) *Institutional Rites and Rights: A Century of Childhood*. London: Institute of Education, University of London.

Alexander, Robin (1999) 'Culture in pedagogy, pedagogy across cultures', in R. Alexander, P. Broadfoot and D. Phillips (eds), *Learning from Comparing: New Directions in Comparative Educational Research. Vol. 1. Contexts, classrooms and outcomes*. Oxford: Symposium. pp. 149–80.

Alexander, Robin (2004) 'Still no pedagogy? Principle, pragmatism and compliance in primary education', *Cambridge Journal of Education*, 34 (1): 7–33.

Alfassi, Miriam (2004) 'Effects of a learner-centred environment on the academic competence and motivation of students at risk', *Learning Environments Research*, 7: 1–22.

Areglado, Ronald J.; Bradley, R.C. and Lane, Pamela S. (1997) *Learning for Life: Creating Classrooms for Self-Directed Learning*. Thousand Oaks CA: Corwin Press.

Arends, Richard I. (2004) *Learning to Teach*. Boston, MA: McGraw Hill.

Aronson, Eliot (n.d.) *Basic Jigsaw 1: Classroom Competition and Cultural Diversity*. www.jigsaw.org/pdf/basics.pdf.

Aronson, Eliot and Bridgeman, Diane (1979) 'Jigsaw groups and the desegregated classroom: In pursuit of common goals', *Personality and Social Psychology Bulletin*, 5: 438–46.

Aronson, Eliot; Blaney, N.; Stephan, C.; Sikes, J. and Snapp, M. (1978) *The Jigsaw Classroom*. Beverly Hills, CA: Sage.

Aronson, Eliot and Patnoe, Shelley (1997) *The Jigsaw Classroom: Building Cooperation in the Classroom*. New York: Allyn & Bacon.

Askew, Sue (ed.) (2000) *Feedback for Learning*. London: Routledge.

Assor, Avi; Kaplan, Haya and Roth, Guy (2002) 'Choice is good, but relevance is excellent: Autonomy-enhancing and suppressing teacher behaviours predicting students' engagement in schoolwork', *British Journal of Educational Psychology*, 72: 261–78.

Atkinson, E. Stephanie (1999) 'Key factors influencing pupil motivation in design and technology', *Journal of Technology Education*, 10 (2): 4–26.

Ball, Stephen J. (1998) 'Educational studies, policy entrepreneurship and social theory', in R. Slee, G. Weiner and S. Tomlinson (eds), *School Effectiveness for Whom? Challenges to the School Effectiveness and School Improvement Movements*. London: Falmer Press.

Baron, Joan Boykoff (1998) 'Using learner-centered assessment on a large scale', in N.M. Lambert and B.L. McCombs (eds), *How Students Learn: Reforming Schools through Learner-centred Education*. Washington DC: American Psychological Association. pp. 211–40.

Bennett, Neville and Dunne, Elisabeth (1992) *Managing Classroom Groups*. Hemel Hempstead: Simon and Schuster.

Benware, Carl A. and Deci, Edward L. (1984) 'Quality of learning with an active versus passive motivational set', *American Educational Research Journal*, 21: 755–65.

Bereiter, Carl and Scardamalia, Marlene (1987) *The Psychology of Written Composition*. Hillsdale, NJ: Lawrence Erlbaum.

Bereiter, Carl and Scardamalia, Marlene (1989) 'Intentional learning as a goal of instruction', in L.B. Resnick (ed.), *Knowing, Learning, and Instruction: Essays in Honor of Robert Glaser*. Hillsdale, NJ: Lawrence Erlbaum. pp. 361–92.

Berliner, David C. (2001) 'Learning about and learning from expert teachers', *International Journal of Educational Research*, 35: 463–82.

Biemans, Harm J.A. and Simons, P. Robert-Jan (1995) 'How to use preconceptions? The CONTACT strategy dismantled', *European Journal of Psychology of Education*, 10: 243–59.

Biggs, John B. (1985) 'The role of metalearning in study processes', *British Journal of Educational Psychology*, 55: 185–212.

Biggs, John B. and Moore, Phillip J. (1993) *The Process of Learning*. Englewood Cliffs, NJ: Prentice-Hall.

Black, Paul (2005) 'The reliability of assessments', in J. Gardner (ed.), *Assessment and Learning: Theory, Policy and Practice*. London: Sage Publications. pp. 119–32.

Black, Paul and Harrison, Christine (2001) 'Self- and peer-assessment and taking responsibility: the science student's role in formative assessment', *School Science Review*, 83 (302): 43–9.

Boggiano, Ann K. and Katz, Phyllis A. (1991) 'Maladaptive achievement patterns in students: the role of teachers' controlling strategies', *Journal of Social Issues*, 47 (4): 35–51.

Boggiano, Ann K; Flink, Cheryl; Shields, Ann; Seelbach, Aubyn and Barrett,

Marty (1993) 'Use of techniques promoting students self-determination: effects on students' analytic problem-solving skills', *Motivation and Emotion*, 17: 319–36.

Boggiano, Ann K; Main, Deborah S. and Katz, Phyllis A. (1988) 'Children's preference for challenge: the role of perceived competence and control', *Journal of Personality and Social Psychology*, 54 (1): 134–41.

Bonnell, Zoe (2005) 'How can the approaches of effective learning help young children learn?' Dissertation for MA in Effective Learning, University of London, Institute of Education.

Bossert, Steven T (1977) 'Tasks, group management, and teacher control behavior: a study of classroom organization and teacher style', *School Review*, 85: 552–65.

Brimblecombe, Nicola; Ormston, Michael and Shaw, Marian (1996) 'Teachers' perceptions of inspections', in J. Ouston, P. Earley and B. Fidler (eds), *OfSTED Inspections: The Early Experience*. London: David Fulton.

Brown, Ann L. (1975) 'The development of memory: knowing, knowing about knowing, and knowing how to know', in H.W. Reese (ed.), *Advances in Child Development and Behavior*. New York: Academic Press.

Brown, Ann L. (1997) 'Transforming schools into communities of thinking and learning about serious matters', *American Psychologist*, 52 (4): 399–413.

Brown, Ann L. and Campione, Joseph C. (1994) 'Guided discovery in a community of learners', in K. McGilly (ed.), *Classroom Lessons: Integrating Cognitive Theory and Classroom Practice*. Cambridge, MA: MIT Press. pp. 229–70.

Brown, Ann L. and Campione, Joseph C. (1998) 'Designing a community of young learners: theoretical and practical lessons', in N.M. Lambert and B.L. McCombs (eds), *How Students Learn: Reforming Schools through Learner-centred Education*. Washington, DC: American Psychological Association. p. 540.

Brown, Carol J. and Fouts, Jeffrey T. (2003) 'Teaching Attributes Observation Protocol', in C.J. Brown and J.T. Fouts (eds), *Classroom Instruction in Achievers Grantee High Schools: A Baseline Report Prepared for the Bill & Melinda Gates Foundation*. Mill Creek, WA: Fouts & Associates.

Bruner, Jerome S. (1996) *The Culture of Education*. Cambridge, MA: Harvard University Press.

Campaign for Learning (2006) *Learning to Learn Project*. Available at http://www.campaign-for-learning.org.uk/projects/L2L/The Project/Project.htm

Campbell, R.J.; Kyriakides, L.; Muijs, R.D. and Robinson, W. (2003) 'Differential teacher effectiveness: towards a model for research and teacher appraisal', *Oxford Review of Education*, 29 (3): 347–62.

Carnell, Eileen (1999) 'Understanding teachers' professional development: an investigation into teachers' learning and their learning contexts'. PhD, University of London, Institute of Education.

Carnell, Eileen (2000) 'Developing learning-centred professional practice', *Professional Development Today*, 3 (3): 21–32.

Carnell, Eileen (2001) 'The value of meta-learning dialogue', *Professional Development Today*, 4: 43–54.

Carnell, Eileen (2004) *'It's like mixing colours', How young people in Year 8 view their learning within the context of the Key Stage 3 National Strategy*. London: Association of Teachers and Lecturers.

Carnell, Eileen (2005) 'Understanding and enriching young people's learning: issues, complexities and challenges', *Improving Schools*, 8 (3): 269–84.

Carnell, Eileen and Lodge, Caroline (2002a) *Supporting Effective Learning*. London: Paul Chapman.

Carnell, Eileen and Lodge, Caroline (2002b) 'Teachers talking about learning: developing richer discourses with young people', *Professional Development Today*, 5 (3): 63–74.

Chalmers, Christina and Nason, Rod (2003) 'Developing primary students' group metacognitive processes in a computer supported collaborative learning environment'. Paper presented at the Joint Conference of the Australian and New Zealand Associations for Research in Education, Auckland, NZ.

Chan, Victoria (2001) 'Learning autonomously: the learners' perspectives', *Journal of Further and Higher Education*, 25 (3): 285–300.

Chapman, Christopher (2001) 'Changing classrooms through inspection', *School Leadership & Management*, 21 (1): 59–73.

Charles, Nickila L. (2004) 'Meaningful marking: a research study that explores how effectively focused marking can improve students' understanding and awareness of their learning'. Dissertation for MA in School Effectiveness and School Improvement, University of London, Institute of Education.

Chi, Michelene T.H. (1996) 'Constructing self-explanations and scaffolded explanations in tutoring', *Applied Cognitive Psychology*, 10 (SISI): S33–S49.

Chi, Michelene T.H.; de Leeuw, Nicholas; Chiu, Mei-Hung and LaVancher, Christian (1994) 'Eliciting self-explanations improves understanding', *Cognitive Science*, 18: 439–77.

Clarke, Shirley (2001) *Unlocking Formative Assessment: Practical Strategies for Enhancing Pupils' Learning in the Primary Classroom*. Hodder & Stoughton Educational.

Claxton, Guy (1999) *Wise Up: The Challenge of Lifelong Learning*. London: Bloomsbury.

Cochran-Smith, Marilyn and Lytle, Susan (1993) *Inside/Outside: Teacher Research and Knowledge*. New York: Teachers College Press.

Coffield, Frank (2005) *Learning Style Questionnaires more Hindrance than Help*. Press release 10 November. London: University of London Institute of Education.

Coffield, Frank; Moseley, David; Hall, Elaine and Ecclestone, Kathryn (2004a) *Should We Be Using Learning Styles? What Research has to say to Practice*. London: Learning and Skills Research Centre.

Coffield, Frank; Moseley, David; Hall, Elaine and Ecclestone, Kathryn (2004b)

Learning Styles and Pedagogy in Post-16 Learning: A Systematic and Critical Review. London: Learning and Skills Research Centre.

Cohen, Elizabeth G. (1992) 'Conditions for productive small groups', in F.M. Newmann (ed.), *Issues in Restructuring Schools. Issue Report No 2: Making Small Groups Productive*. Madison, WI: University of Wisconsin Center on Organization and Restructuring of Schools.

Cohen, Elizabeth G. (1994) *Designing Groupwork: Strategies for the Heterogeneous Classroom*. New York: Teachers College Press.

Collins, Cathy and Mangieri, John N. (eds) (1992) *Teaching Thinking: An Agenda for the 21st Century*. Hillsdale, NJ: Lawrence Erlbaum.

Cooper, Paul and McIntyre, Donald (1993) 'Commonality in teachers' and pupils' perceptions of effective classroom learning', *BJEP*, 63 (3): 381–99.

Corno, Lyn (1992) 'Encouraging students to take responsibility for learning and performance', *Elementary School Journal*, 93 (1): 69–83

Costa, Arthur L. and Kallick, Bena (2000) *Habits of Mind: A Developmental Series. Book III: Assessing and Reporting Growth in Habits of Mind*. Alexandria, VA: Association for Supervision and Curriculum Development.

Cotton, Chris; Creasy, Jane; Kennedy, Howard and West-Burnham, John (2003) *'New Visions' Programme for Early Headship*. Nottingham: National College for School Leadership.

Cowie, Helen and Rudduck, Jean (1990) *Co-operative Learning: Traditions and Transitions*. London: BP Educational Service on behalf of the Co-operative Group Work Project at Sheffield University.

Crook, Charles (1999) 'Motivation and the ecology of collaborative learning', in R. Joiner, K. Littleton, D. Faulkner and D. Miell (eds), *Rethinking Collaborative Learning*. London: Free Association Books. pp. 161–78.

Cuttance, Peter (1998) 'Quality assurance reviews as a catalyst for school improvement in Australia', in A. Hargreaves, A. Lieberman, M. Fullan and D. Hopkins (eds), *International Handbook of Educational Change (Part Two)*. Dordrecht: Kluwer. pp. 1135–62.

Daniels, Denise Honeycutt and Perry, Kathryn E. (2003) *'"Learner-centered" according to children'*, *Theory Into Practice*, 42 (2): 102–8.

Daniels, Denise Honeycutt; Kalkman, Deborah L. and McCombs, Barbara L. (2001) 'Young children's perceptions on learning and teacher practices in different classroom contexts: implications for motivation', *Early Education and Development*, 12 (2): 253–73.

Darling-Hammond, Linda and Falk, Beverly (1997) 'Using standards and assessments to support student learning', *Phi Delta Kappan*, 79 (3): 190–99.

Daukes, Julie (2004) 'When we listen to children what do we hear? Using the children's voices as a medium for reflection on practice and change'. Assignment for MA in School Effectiveness and School Improvement, Institute of Education, University of London.

de Baessa, Yetilú; Chesterfield, Ray and Ramos, Tanya (2002) 'Active learning and democratic behaviour in Guatemalan rural primary schools', *Compare*, 32 (2): 205–18.

Deci, Edward L. and Ryan, Richard M. (1982) 'Intrinsic motivation to teach: possibilities and obstacles in our colleges and universities', in J. Bess (ed.), *New Directions for Learning and Teaching: Motivating Professors to Teach Effectively*. San Francisco, CA: Jossey-Bass.

Deci, Edward L., Koestner, Richard and Ryan, Richard M. (2001) 'Extrinsic rewards and intrinsic motivation in education: reconsidered once again', *Review of Educational Research*, 71 (1): 1–27.

Deci, Edward L.; Spiegel, Nancy H.; Ryan, Richard M.; Koestner, R. and Kauffmann, Manette (1982) 'The effects of performance standards on teaching styles: the behavior of controlling teachers', *Journal of Educational Psychology*, 74: 852–9.

Dennison, Bill and Kirk, Roger (1990) *Do Review Learn Apply: A Simple Guide to Experiential Learning*. Oxford: Blackwell.

Dewey, John (1916) *Democracy and Education*. New York: Macmillan.

DfES (2004a) *Pedagogy and Practice: Teaching and Learning in Secondary Schools. Unit 19: Learning styles*. London: DfES (Department for Education and Skills).

DfES (2004b) *Standards Site: Personalised Learning: Effective teaching and learning*. Available at
http://www.standards.dfes.gov.uk/personalisedlearning/five/teachinglearning/

Doan, Jane and Chase, Penelle (1996) *Choosing to Learn: Ownership and Responsibility in a Primary Multi-age Classroom*. Portsmouth, NH: Heinemann.

Donoahue, Zoe (2003) 'Science teaching and learning: teachers and children plan together', *Networks Journal*, 6 (1).

Doyle, Lesley and Godfrey, Ray (2005) 'Investigating the reliability of the Key Stage 2 test results for assessing individual pupil achievement and progress in England', *London Review of Education*, 3 (1): 29–45.

Duffield, Jill; Allan, Julie; Turner, Eileen and Morris, Brian (2000) 'Pupils' voices on achievement: an alternative to the standards agenda', *Cambridge Journal of Education*, 30 (2): 263–74.

Dweck, Carol S. (1999) *Self-Theories: Their Role in Motivation, Personality, and Development*. Philadelphia, PA: Psychology Press.

Ertmer, Peggy A. and Newby, Timothy J. (1996) 'The expert learner: strategic, self-regulated, and reflective', *Instructional Science*, 24 (1): 1–24.

Fielding, Michael (2004) 'Transformative approaches to student voice: theoretical underpinnings, recalcitrant realities', *British Educational Research Journal*, 30 (2): 295–311.

Flavell, John H. (1976) 'Metacognitive aspects of problem-solving', in L.B. Resnick (ed.), *The Nature of Intelligence*. Hillsdale, NJ: Lawrence Erlbaum. pp. 231–5.

Flink, Cheryl; Boggiano, Ann K. and Barrett, Marty (1990) 'Controlling teaching strategies: undermining children's self-determination and performance', *Jour-*

nal of Personality and Social Psychology, 59: 916–24.

Fortier, Michelle S; Vallerand, Robert J. and Guay, Frédéric (1995) 'Academic motivation and school performance: toward a structural model', *Contemporary Educational Psychology*, 20 (3): 257–74.

Freire, Paulo (1970) *Pedagogy of the Oppressed*. London: Penguin.

Galton, Maurice and Williamson, John (1992) *Group Work in the Primary Classroom*. London: Routledge.

Gardner, Howard; Csikszentmihalyi, Mihaly and Damon, William (2001) *Good Work: When Excellence and Ethics Meet*. New York: Basic Books.

Gardner, John and Cowan, Pamela (2005) 'The fallibility of high stakes "11-plus" testing in Northern Ireland', *Assessment in Education*, 12 (2): 145–65.

Geist, Eugene and Baum, Angela C. (2005) 'Yeah, Buts that keep teachers from embracing an active curriculum: overcoming the resistance', *Young Children*, (July): www.journal.naeyc.org/btj/200507/03Geist.pdf

Getzels, Jacob W. (1977) 'Images of the classroom and visions of the learner', in J.C. Glidewell (ed.), *The Social Context of Learning and Development*. New York: Gardner Press.

Gibbs, Graham (1981) *Teaching Students to Learn: A Student-centred Approach*. Milton Keynes: Open University Press.

Gibbs, Graham (1986) *Learning to Study*. Available from National Extension College, 18 Brooklands Avenue, Cambridge CB2 2HN.

Gibbs, Graham (1988) *Learning by Doing: A Guide to Teaching and Learning Methods*. London: Further Education Unit.

Gokhale, Anuradha A. (1995) 'Collaborative learning enhances critical thinking', *Journal of Technology Education*, 7(1).

Good, Thomas L.; Slavings, Ricky L.; Harel, Kathleen Hobson and Emerson, Hugh (1987) 'Student passivity: a study of question asking in K-12 classrooms', *Sociology of Education*, 60 (3): 181–99.

Gray, John; Hopkins, David; Reynolds, David; Wilcox, Brian; Farrell, Shaun and Jesson, David (1999) *Improving Schools: Performance and Potential*. Buckingham: Open University Press.

GTCE (2004) 2004 *Survey of Teachers*. London: NFER/General Teaching Council for England.

Guay, Frédéric and Vallerand, Robert J. (1997) 'Social context, students' motivation, and academic achievement: toward a process model', *Social Psychology of Education*, 1: 211–33.

Haller, Eileen P.; Child, David A. and Walberg, Herbert J. (1988) 'Can comprehension be taught? A quantitative synthesis of "metacognitive" studies', *Educational Researcher*, 17 (9): 5–8.

Halpern, Diane F. (1998) 'Teaching critical thinking for transfer across domains: dispositions, skills, structure training, and metacognitive monitoring', *American Psychologist*, 53 (4): 449–55.

Hammond, Sue Annis (2000) *The Thin Book of Appreciative Inquiry*. Bend, OR:

www.thinbook.com

Hammond, Sue Annis and Mayfield, Andrea B. (2004) *The Thin Book of Naming Elephants: How to Surface Undiscussables for Greater Organizational Success*. Bend, OR: www.thinbook.com

Hargreaves, David H. (2004) *About Learning: Report of the Learning Working Group*. London: Demos.

Hargreaves, Eleanore (2005) 'Assessment for learning? Thinking outside the (black) box', *Cambridge Journal of Education*, 35 (2): 213–24.

Harlen, Wynn and Deakin-Crick, Ruth (2002) *A Systematic Review of the Impact of Summative Assessment and Tests on Students' Motivation for Learning*. London: EPPI-Centre, Social Science Research Unit, University of London Institute of Education.

Harris, Dean (2002) 'Children's conceptions of learning: an investigation into what children think learning is in three contrasting schools'. Dissertation for MA in Effective Learning, University of London Institute of Education.

Hart, Susan; Dixon, Annabelle; Drummond, Mary Jane and McIntyre, Donald (2004) *Learning Without Limits*. Buckingham: Open University Press.

Hattie, John; Biggs, John and Purdie, Nola (1996) 'Effects of learning skills interventions on student learning: a meta-analysis', *Review of Educational Research*, 66 (2): 99–136.

Heo, Heeok (2000) 'Theoretical underpinnings for structuring the classroom as self-regulated learning environment', *Educational Technology International*, 3 (1): 31–51.

Hiebert, James; Gallimore, Ronald; Garnier, Helen; Givvin, Karen Bogard; Hollingsworth, Hilary; Jacobs, Jennifer; Chui, Angel Miu-Ying; Wearne, Diana; Smith, Margaret; Kersting, Nicole; Manaster, Alfred; Tseng, Ellen; Etterbeek, Wallace; Manaster, Carl; Gonzales, Patrick and Stigler, James (2003) *Teaching Mathematics in Seven Countries: Results From the TIMSS 1999 Video Study*. Washington, DC: US Department of Education National Center for Education Statistics.

Higgins, Karen M.; Harris, Nancy A. and Kuehn, Laura L. (1994) 'Placing assessment into the hands of young children: a study of student-generated criteria and self-assessment', *Educational Assessment*, 2 (4): 309–24.

Hofstede, Geert (1980) *Culture's Consequences: International Differences in Work Related Values*. London: Sage.

Hogan, Kathleen (1999) 'Thinking aloud together: a test of an intervention to foster students' collaborative scientific reasoning', *Journal of Research in Science Teaching*, 36 (10): 1085–109.

Holt, John (1991) *Learning All the Time*. Ticknall: Education Now.

Hong Kong Education Department (2002) *Basic Education Curriculum Guide*. Hong Kong: Education and Manpower Bureau.

Hughes, Mike (1993) *Flexible Learning: Evidence Examined*. Stafford: Network Educational Press.

Hughes, Mike (1997) *Lessons are for Learning.* Stafford: Network Educational Press.

Hughes, Mike (2002) *Tweak to Transform: A Practical Handbook for School Leaders.* Stafford: Network Educational Press.

Inagaki, Kayoko; Hatano, Giyoo and Morita, Eiji (1998) 'Construction of mathematical knowledge through whole-class discussion', *Learning and Instruction*, 8 (6): 503–26.

Ireson, Judy and Hallam, Susan (2001) *Ability Grouping in Education.* London: Sage.

Jacob, Evelyn (1999) *Cooperative Learning In Context: An Educational Innovation in Everyday Classrooms.* New York: SUNY Press.

James, Mary (2006) 'Learning how to learn in classrooms, schools and networks'. Paper presented at the ESRC Learning to Learn network meeting: 7 July 2005, Institute of Education.

Jeffers, Susan (1997) *Feel the Fear and Do It Anyway.* London: Rider & Co.

Johnson, David W.; Johnson, Roger T. and Smith, Karl A. (1991) *Active Learning: Cooperation in the College Classroom.* Edina, MN: Interaction Book Company.

Kane, Liam (2004) 'Educators, learners and active learning methodologies', *International Journal of Lifelong Education*, 23 (3): 275–86.

Kaplan, Avi and Midgley, Carol (1999) 'The relationship between perceptions of the classroom goal structure and early adolescents' affect in school: the mediating role of coping strategies', *Learning and Individual Differences*, 11 (2): 187–212.

Kaplan, Avi; Gheen, Margaret and Midgley, Carol (2002) 'Classroom goal structure and student disruptive behaviour', *British Journal of Educational Psychology*, 72: 191–211.

Kelly, Marie; Moore, Dennis W.; and Tuck, Bryan F. (1994) 'Reciprocal teaching in a regular primary school classroom', *Journal of Educational Research*, 88 (1): 53–61.

King, Alison (1993) 'From sage on the stage to guide on the side', *College Teaching*, 41 (1): 30–5.

King, Alison (1994) 'Guiding knowledge construction in the classroom: effects of teaching children how to question and how to explain', *American Educational Research Journal*, 31 (2): 358–68.

King, Alison and Rosenshine, Barak (1993) 'Effects of guided cooperative questioning on children's knowledge construction', *Journal of Experimental Education*, 61(2): 127–48.

King, Alison; Staffieri, Anne and Adelgais, Anne (1998) 'Mutual peer tutoring: effects of structuring tutorial interaction to scaffold peer learning', *Journal of Educational Psychology*, 90 (1): 134–52.

Klenowski, Val; Askew, Sue and Carnell, Eileen (2006) 'Portfolios for learning, assessment and professional development in higher education', *Assessment and Evaluation in Higher Education*, 31: 267–96.

Kolb, David A. (1984) *Experiential Learning: Experience as the Source of Learning and Development*. Englewood Cliffs, NJ: Prentice-Hall.

Kuhn, Deanna and Pearsall, Susan (1998) 'Relations between metastrategic knowledge and strategic performance', *Cognitive Development*, 13 (2): 227–47.

Kurz, Yvonne (2003) 'An exploration of different feedback strategies in a London primary school, and the effects they have on future learning'. Report for MA in Effective Learning, University of London Institute of Education.

Kutnick, Peter; Sebba, Judy; Blatchford, Peter; Galton, Maurice and Thorp, Jo (2005) *The Effects of Pupil Grouping: Literature Review. Research Report RR688*. London: DfES.

Lambert, Nadine M. and McCombs, Barbara L. (1998) 'Learner-centered schools and classrooms as a direction for school reform', in N.M. Lambert and B.L. McCombs (eds), *How Students Learn: Reforming Schools through Learner-centred Education*. Washington, DC: American Psychological Association. pp. 1–22.

Lawrence, Jean; Steed, David and Young, Pam (1989) *Disruptive Pupils – Disruptive Schools?* London: Routledge.

Levin, Benjamin (2000) 'Putting students at the centre in education reform', *Journal of Educational Change*, 1 (2): 155–72.

Lodge, Caroline (2002) 'An investigation into discourses of learning in schools'. EdD thesis, University of London Institute of Education.

Lodge, Caroline (2003) '"The questions they ask!" Teachers and students talk about learning'. Paper presented at the International Congress of School Effectiveness and Improvement, Sydney, Australia.

Lodge, Caroline (2005) 'From hearing voices to engaging in dialogue: problematising student participation in school improvement', *Journal of Educational Change*, 6: 125–46.

Lodge, Caroline (forthcoming) 'Regarding learning: children's drawings of learning in the classroom', *Learning Environments Research*.

Lyman, Frank T. (1981) 'The responsive classroom discussion', in A.S. Anderson (ed.), *Mainstreaming Digest*. College Park, MD: University of Maryland College of Education. pp. 109–13.

MacIntosh, Shona (2005) 'Is it possible to build a learning community in a highly competitive secondary school environment?' Dissertation for MA in Effective Learning, University of London Institute of Education.

Maharasingam, Naheeda (2004) 'Learning journals: a journey to promote richer conceptions of learning'. Report for MA in Effective Learning, University of London Institute of Education.

Marble, Stephen; Finley, Sandra and Ferguson, Chris (2000) *Understanding Teachers' Perspectives on Teaching and Learning: A Synthesis of Work in Five Study Sites*. Austin, TX: Southwest Educational Developmental Laboratory.

Martin, Elaine and Ramsden, Paul (1987) 'Learning skills or skill in learning?' in J. Richardson, M. Eysenck and D. Warren Piper (eds), *Student Learning: Research in Education and Cognitive Psychology*. Milton Keynes: SRHE/Open University Press.

Marton, Ference; Dall'Alba, Gloria and Beaty, Elizabeth (1993) 'Conceptions of learning', *International Journal of Educational Research*, 19 (3): 277–300.

Mayer, Richard E. (1998) 'Cognitive theory for education: what teachers need to know', in N.M. Lambert and B.L. McCombs (eds), *How Students Learn: Reforming Schools through Learner-centred Education*. Washington, DC: American Psychological Association. pp. 353–78.

Mayer, Richard E. (2001) 'Changing conceptions of learning: a century of progress in the scientific study of education', in L. Corno (ed.), *Education across a Century: 100th Yearbook of the NSSE*. Chicago, IL: University of Chicago Press.

McCarthy, J. Patrick and Anderson, Liam (2000) 'Active learning techniques versus traditional teaching styles: two experiments from history and political science', *Innovative Higher Education*, 24 (4): 279–91.

McManus, Susan M. and Gettinger, Maribeth (1996) 'Teacher and student evaluations of cooperative learning and observed interactive behaviors', *Journal of Educational Research*, 90 (1): 13–22.

McNeil, Linda M. (1988) 'Contradictions of control. Part 1: Administrators and teachers; Part 2: Teachers, students, and curriculum; Part 3: Contradictions of reform', *Phi Delta Kappan*, 69: 333–9, 432–8, 478–85.

Meece, Judith L. (2003) 'Applying learner-centered principles to middle school education', *Theory into Practice*, 42 (2): 109–16.

Meece, Judith L.; Herman, Phillip and McCombs, Barbara L. (2003) 'Relations of learner-centered teaching practices to adolescents' achievement goals', *International Journal of Educational Research*, 39: 457–75.

Mercer, Neil (2002) 'Developing dialogues', in G. Wells and G. Claxton, (eds), *Learning for Life in the 21st Century: Sociocultural Perspectives on the Future of Education*. Oxford: Blackwell. pp. 73–83.

Michaelsen, Larry K. (1999) 'Myths and methods in successful small group work', *National Teaching & Learning Forum*, 8 (6).

Moore, Alex (2004) *The Good Teacher: Dominant Discourses in Teaching and Teacher Education*. London: RoutledgeFalmer.

Munro, John (1999) 'Learning more about learning improves teacher effectiveness', *School Effectiveness and School Improvement*, 10 (2): 151–71.

Murphy, Patricia and Hennessy, Sara (2001) 'Realising the potential – and lost opportunities – for peer collaboration in a D&T setting', *International Journal of Technology and Design Education*, 11 (3): 203–37.

National Center for Research on Teacher Learning (1993) *How Teachers Learn to Engage Students in Active Learning*. East Lansing, MI: National Center for Research on Teacher Learning, Michigan State University.

Newmann, Fred M.; Bryk, Anthony S. and Nagaoka, Jenny K. (2001) *Authentic Intellectual Work and Standardized Tests: Conflict or Coexistence?* Chicago, IL: Consortium on Chicago School Research.

Nias, Jennifer (2000) 'Preface', in A. Pollard and P. Triggs (eds), *What Children*

Say: Changing Policy and Practice in Primary Education. London: Continuum.

Nichols, Sharon L. and Berliner, David C. (2005) *The Inevitable Corruption of Indicators and Educators Through High-Stakes Testing*. Tempe, AZ: Arizona State University Education Policy Studies Laboratory.

Niemi, Hannele (2002) 'Active learning: a cultural change needed in teacher education and schools', *Teaching and Teacher Education*, 18: 763–80.

Nisbet, John and Shucksmith, Janet (1984) *The Seventh Sense: Reflections on Learning to Learn*. Edinburgh: Scottish Council for Research in Education.

Novak, Joseph D. and Gowin, D. Bob (1984) *Learning How to Learn*. Cambridge: Cambridge University Press.

OECD (1993) *Teacher Quality: New Ways of Teaching and Learning*. Paris: OECD (Organisation for Economic Co-operation and Development) Centre for Educational Research and Innovation.

OECD (2001a) *Knowledge and Skills for Life: First Results from the OECD 'Programme for International Student Assessment'* (PISA) 2000. Paris: OECD (Organisation for Economic Co-operation and Development).

OECD (2001b) *Schooling for Tomorrow: What Schools for the Future?* Paris: OECD (Organisation for Economic Co-operation and Development) Centre for Educational Research and Innovation.

Ofsted (2003) *Inspecting Schools: Framework for Inspecting Schools*. London: Office for Standards in Education.

Olson, David R. (2003) *Psychological Theory and Educational Reform: How School Remakes Mind and Society*. Cambridge: Cambridge University Press.

Palincsar, AnneMarie Sullivan and Brown, Ann L. (1984) 'Reciprocal teaching of comprehension-fostering and monitoring activities', *Cognition and Instruction*, 1: 117–75.

Panitz, Theodore (1999) 'The motivational benefits of cooperative learning', *New Directions for Teaching and Learning*, (78): 59–67.

Panitz, Theodore (2000) '67 Benefits of cooperative learning'. Available at http://home.capecod.net/~tpanitz/tedsarticles/coopbenefits.htm

Paris, Cynthia and McCombs, Barbara (2000) 'Teachers' perspectives on what it means to be learner-centered'. Paper presented at the Annual meeting of the American Educational Research Association, New Orleans.

Paris, Scott G. and Paris, Alison H. (2001) 'Classroom applications of research on self-regulated learning', *Educational Psychologist*, 36 (2): 89–101.

Passe, Jeff (1996) *When Students Choose Content: A Guide to Increasing Motivation, Autonomy, and Achievement*. Thousand Oaks, CA: Corwin Press.

Pelletier, Luc G.; Séguin-Lévesque, Chantal and Legault, Louise (2002) 'Pressure from above and pressure from below as determinants of teachers' motivation and teaching behaviors', *Journal of Educational Psychology*, 94 (1): 186–96.

Perkins, David N. (1993) *Thinking Connections: Learning to Think and Thinking to Learn*. Menlo Park, CA: Addison-Wesley.

Perrone, Vita (1994) 'How to engage students in learning', *Educational Leadership*, 51 (5): 11–13.

Peterson, Penelope L.; Carpenter, Thomas P. and Fennema, Elizabeth (1989) 'Teachers' knowledge of students' knowledge in mathematics problem-solving: correlational and case analyses', *Journal of Educational Psychology*, 81: 558–69.

Pollard, Andrew and Triggs, P (eds) (2000) *What Children Say: Changing Policy and Practice in Primary Education*. London: Continuum.

Pramling, Ingrid (1990) *Learning to Learn: A Study of Swedish Preschool Children*. New York: Springer-Verlag.

Pratton, Jerry and Hales, Loyde W. (1986) 'The effects of active participation on student learning', *Journal of Educational Research*, 79 (4): 210–15.

Qualters, Donna M. (2001) 'Do students want to be active?' *Journal of Scholarship of Teaching and Learning*, 2 (1): 51–60.

Ramsay, Peter (1993) *Teacher Quality: New Zealand report for the OECD/CERI study on Teacher Quality*. Paris: OECD (Organisation for Economic Co-operation and Development) Centre for Educational Research and Innovation.

Reay, Diane and Wiliam, Dylan (1999) '"I'll be a nothing": structure, agency and the construction of identity through assessment', *British Educational Research Journal*, 25 (3): 343–54.

Reed, Jane (2004) *Dorset Primary Improvement in Action Project*. London: Institute of Education, University of London. International School Effectiveness and Improvement Centre.

Reeve, Johnmarshall (2006) 'Teachers as facilitators: what autonomy-supportive teachers do and why their students benefit', *The Elementary School Journal*, 106: 225–36.

Reeve, Johnmarshall; Bolt, Elizabeth and Cai, Yi (1999) 'Autonomy-supportive teachers: how they teach and motivate students', *Journal of Educational Psychology*, 91 (3): 537–48.

Reeve, Johnmarshall; Jang, Hyungshim; Carrell, Dan; Jeon, Soohyun and Barch, Jon (2004) 'Enhancing students' engagement by increasing teachers' autonomy support', *Motivation and Emotion*, 28 (2): 147–69.

Richards, C. (2000) 'Testing, testing, testing', *Education Journal*, 46, June: 19.

Robinson, Francis P. (1970) *Effective Study*. New York: Harper and Row.

Robinson, W. Lewis (1974) 'Conscious competency – the mark of the competent instructor', *Personnel Journal*, 53 (7): 538–9.

Roettger, Doris (1978) 'Reading attitudes and the Estes scale'. Paper presented at the 23rd Convention of the International Reading Association, Houston, Texas.

Rosenholtz, Susan J. (1989) *Teachers' Workplace: The Social Organization of Schools*. New York: Longman.

Rudduck, Jean and Cowie, Helen (1988) *Cooperative Group Work: An Overview*. London: BP Educational Service.

Rudduck, Jean; Chaplain, Roland and Wallace, Gwen (eds) (1996) *School Improvement: What Can Pupils Tell Us?* London: David Fulton.

Ruhl, Kathy L; Hughes, Charles A. and Schloss, Patrick J. (1987) 'Using the pause procedure to enhance lecture recall', *Teacher Education and Special Education*, 10 (Winter): 14–18.

Russell, Bertrand (1926) *On Education*. London: George, Allen & Unwin.

Ryan, Richard M. and Deci, Edward L. (2000) 'Intrinsic and extrinsic motivations: classic definitions and new directions', *Contemporary Educational Psychology*, 25: 54–67.

Ryan, Richard M; Connell, James P. and Deci, Edward L. (1985) 'A motivational analysis of self-determination and self-regulation in education', in C. Ames and R. Ames (eds), *Research on Motivation in Education Vol 2 The Classroom Milieu*. San Diego, CA: Academic Press.

Sachs, Judyth (2000) 'The activist professional', *Journal of Educational Change*, 1 (1): 77–95.

Sanford, Betsy (1988) 'Writing reflectively', *Language Arts*, 65 (7): 652–7.

Sarason, Seymour B. (1990) *The Predictable Failure of Educational Reform*. San Francisco, CA: Jossey-Bass.

Säljö, Roger (1979) 'Learning about learning', *Higher Education*, 8 (4): 443–51.

Scardamalia, Marlene and Bereiter, Carl (1983) 'Child as coinvestigator: helping children gain insight into their own mental processes', in S.G. Paris, G.M. Olson and H.W. Stevenson (eds), *Learning and Motivation in the Classroom*. Hillsdale, NJ: Lawrence Erlbaum.

Scardamalia, Marlene and Bereiter, Carl (1991) 'Higher levels of agency for children in knowledge building: a challenge for the design of new knowledge media', *The Journal of the Learning Sciences*, 1: 37–68.

Scardamalia, Marlene and Bereiter, Carl (1992) 'Text-based and knowledge-based questioning by children', *Cognition and Instruction*, 9 (3): 177–99.

Scardamalia, Marlene; Bereiter, Carl and Steinbach, Rosanne (1984) 'Teachability of reflective processes in written composition', *Cognitive Science*, 8 (2): 173–90.

Schwartz, Daniel L. (1995) 'The emergence of abstract representations in dyad problem solving', *Journal of the Learning Sciences*, 4: 321–54.

Seymour, Jennifer R. and Osana, Helena P. (2003) 'Reciprocal teaching procedures and principles: two teachers' developing understanding', *Teaching and Teacher Education*, 19: 325–44.

Shachar, Hanna and Sharan, Shlomo (1995) 'Cooperative learning and the organization of secondary schools', *School Effectiveness and School Improvement*, 6 (1): 47–66.

Shepard, Lorrie A. (2000) 'The role of assessment in a learning culture', *Educational Researcher*, 29 (7): 4–14.

Shuell, Thomas J. (1986) 'Cognitive conceptions of learning', *Review of Educational Research*, 56 (4): 411–36.

Simons, P. Robert-Jan (1997) 'Definitions and theories of active learning', in D. Stern and G.L. Huber (eds), *Active Learning for Students and Teachers: Reports from Eight Countries*. Frankfurt am Main: OECD/Peter Lang. pp. 19–39.

Singapore Ministry of Education (2002) *Report of the Junior College/Upper Secondary Education Review Committee*. Singapore: Ministry of Education.

Sivan, Atara; Leung, Roberta Wong; Woon, Chi-ching and Kember, David (2000) 'An implementation of active learning and its effect on the quality of student learning', *Innovations in Education and Teaching International*, 37 (4): 381–9.

Smith, Mary Lee (1991) 'Meanings of test preparation', *American Educational Research Journal*, 28 (3): 521–42.

Starnes, Bobby Ann and Paris, Cynthia (2000) 'Choosing to learn', *Phi Delta Kappan*, 81 (5): 392–7.

Staub, Fritz C. and Stern, Elsbeth (2002) 'The nature of teachers' pedagogical content beliefs matters for students' achievement gains: quasi-experimental evidence from elementary mathematics', *Journal of Educational Psychology*, 94 (2): 344–55.

Stefani, Lorraine A.J. (1994) 'Peer, self and tutor assessment: relative reliabilities', *Studies in Higher Education*, 19 (1): 69–75.

Stefanou, Candice R; Perencevich, Kathleen C; DiCintio, Matthew and Turner, Julianne C. (2004) 'Supporting autonomy in the classroom: ways teachers encourage student decision making and ownership', *Educational Psychologist*, 39 (2): 97–110.

Sternberg, Robert J. (2003) 'What is an "expert student?"', *Educational Researcher*, 32 (8): 5–9.

Stigler, James W. and Hiebert, James (1998) 'Teaching is a cultural activity', *American Educator*, 22 (4): 4–11.

Stobart, Gordon and Stoll, Louise (2005) 'The Key Stage 3 Strategy: what kind of reform is this?' *Cambridge Journal of Education*, 35 (2): 225–38.

Sullivan, John (2000) 'Stand and deliver – the teacher's integrity?' in C. Watkins, C. Lodge and R. Best (eds), *Tomorrow's Schools – Towards Integrity*. London: Routledge. pp. 78–93.

Thomas, Gregory P. (2003) 'Conceptualisation, development and validation of an instrument for investigating the metacognitive orientation of science classroom learning environments: The Metacognitive Orientation Learning Environment Scale – Science (MOLES-S)', *Learning Environments Research*, 6 (2): 175–97.

Tiessen, Esther L. and Ward, Douglas R. (1997) 'Collaboration by design: context, structure, and medium', *Journal of Interactive Learning Research*, 8 (2): 175–97.

Timbrell, Kirsten (2004) 'Dispelling the "fear factor": an experiment in building a learning community in a classroom'. Assignment for MA in Effective Learning, University of London, Institute of Education.

Troia, Gary A; Graham, Steve and Harris, Karen R. (1999) 'Teaching students with learning disabilities to mindfully plan when writing', *Exceptional Children*, 65: 253–70.

Vallerand, Robert J.; Guay, Frédéric and Fortier, Michelle S. (1997) 'Self-determination and persistence in a real-life setting: toward a motivational model of high school dropout', *Journal of Personality and Social Psychology*, 72 (5): 1161–76.

Vasconcelos, Teresa and Walsh, Daniel J. (2001) 'Conversations around the large table: building community in the daily life of a Portuguese kindergarten', *Early Education and Development*, 12 (4): 499–522.

Vogel, Nancy (2001) *Making the Most of Plan-Do-Review*. Ypsilanti, MI: High/Scope Press.

Vygotsky, Lev S. (1978) *Mind in Society: The Development of Higher Psychological Processes*. Cambridge, MA: Harvard University Press.

Wagner, Patsy and Watkins, Chris (2005) 'Narrative work in schools', in A. Vetere and E. Dowling (eds), *Narrative Therapies with Children and their Families: A Practitioners' Guide to Concepts and Approaches*. Hove: Routledge. pp. 239–53.

Wallace, Belle; Maker, June; Cave, Diana and Chandler, Simon (2004) *Thinking Skills and Problem-Solving: An Inclusive Approach*. London: David Fulton.

Watkins, Chris (2001) *Learning about Learning Enhances Performance (Research Matters Series No. 13)*. London: Institute of Education School Improvement Network.

Watkins, Chris (2003) *Learning: A Sense-maker's Guide*. London: Association of Teachers and Lecturers.

Watkins, Chris (2004) *Classrooms as Learning Communities (Research Matters Series No. 24)*. London: Institute of Education School Improvement Network.

Watkins, Chris (2005) *Classrooms as Learning Communities: What's in it for Schools*. London: Routledge.

Watkins, Chris and Whalley, Caroline (1993) *Mentoring: Resources for School-based Development*. Harlow: Longman.

Watkins, Chris; Carnell, Eileen; Lodge, Caroline; Wagner, Patsy and Whalley, Caroline (2000) *Learning about Learning: Resources for Supporting Effective Learning*. London: Routledge.

Watkins, Chris; Carnell, Eileen; Lodge, Caroline; Wagner, Patsy and Whalley, Caroline (2002) *Effective Learning (Research Matters Series No. 17)*. London: Institute of Education School Improvement Network.

Webb, Noreen M. (1989) 'Peer interaction and learning in small groups', *International Journal of Educational Research*, 13: 21–39.

Webb, Noreen M. and Palincsar, AnneMarie Sullivan (1996) 'Group processes in the classroom', in D.C. Berliner and R.C. Calfee (eds), *Handbook of Educational Psychology*. New York: Simon & Schuster. pp. 841–73.

Webb, Noreen; Nemer, Kariane M; Kersting, Nicole; Ing, Marsha and Forrest, Jeffrey (2004) *The Effects of Teacher Discourse on Student Behavior and Learning in Peer-Directed Groups*. Los Angeles, CA: National Center for Research on Evaluation, Standards, and Student Testing (CRESST)/University of California, Los Angeles.

Weber, Sandra and Mitchell, Claudia (1995) *"That's funny, you don't look like a teacher". Interrogating Images and Identity in Popular Culture.* London: RoutledgeFalmer.

Weimer, Maryellen (2002) *Learner Centered Teaching: Five Key Changes to Practice.* San Francisco, CA: Jossey-Bass.

Weinberger, Elizabeth and McCombs, Barbara L. (2001) 'The impact of learner-centered practices on the academic and non-academic outcomes of upper elementary and middle school students'. Paper presented at the annual meeting of the American Educational Research Association, Seattle.

Wheelock, Anne; Bebell, Damian J. and Haney, Walt (2000) 'What can student drawings tell us about high-stakes testing in Massachusetts?' *Teachers College Record*, available at http://www.tcrecord.org ID Number: 10634.

Whicker, Kristina M; Bol, Linda and Nunnery, John A. (1997) 'Cooperative learning in the secondary mathematics classroom', *The Journal of Educational Research*, 91 (1): 42–8.

White, Michael (1985) 'Fear busting and monster taming: an approach to the fears of young children', *Dulwich Centre Review* 29–34.

White, Richard T. and Gunstone, Richard F. (1989) 'Metalearning and conceptual change', *International Journal of Science Education*, 11 (5): 577–86.

Wiliam, Dylan (2001) 'Reliability, validity and all that jazz', *Education 3–13*, 29 (3): 17–21.

Williams, Emma (2002) 'Enriched learning narratives'. Dissertation for MA in School Effectiveness and School Improvement, University of London, Institute of Education.

Wolters, Christopher A; Yu, Shirley L. and Pintrich, Paul R. (1996) 'The relation between goal orientation and students' motivational beliefs and self-regulated learning', *Learning And Individual Differences*, 8 (3): 211–38.

Wrigley, Terry (2000) 'Misunderstanding school improvement', *Improving Schools*, 3 (1): 23–9.

Yair, Gad (2000) 'Reforming motivation: how the structure of instruction affects students' learning experiences', *British Educational Research Journal*, 26 (2): 191–210.

Author index